D1606157

The Red Feathered Soul and Other Angels in Flight

True Stories of Visits From Loved Ones Passed On

Lori Baker

Forward

       After losing seven of the souls she was closest to within a two-year time period, the author found this part of her journey with grief to be such a lonely walk. Yet at the same time, she saw miracles start to happen when she first asked her mother to visit as a cardinal. Soon after the first visit, poems came to her through spirit. After sharing these poems, she found so many people had such beautiful and amazing stories of their loved ones coming to visit at the exact moment they needed them, or in a moment they knew their loved ones were cheering them on. All came through other angels in flight, such as the bluejay, butterfly, hummingbird, dragonfly, seagull, waterbird, etc. They also appeared as angel signs such as feathers, coins, songs from their past and other amazing synchronicities. Turning her pain into purpose, this became a passion and mission for her to help others grieving. These amazing true stories will be sure to bring you peace, love and connection. Love truly never dies. There are indeed signs from our loved ones everywhere.

Table of Contents

Contributions and Dedications

Credits - Graphic Design, Layout, and Editing - Kenjie Ordoñez

Editing – Annie Joy

Watercolor Artists - Maria Stezhko, Yuliya Derbisheva, Lorri Kajenna, Amber Sun, Silmairel

Special thank you to all those who opened their hearts and shared their stories. Nellie Davis of the Facebook Group "Anything Cardinals" for allowing me to post and share my story, and for creating such a loving community. Kenjie Ordoñez, thank you for your magic, your vision, and your belief. You are beyond talented. Thank you to the most amazing and gifted watercolor artists Maria Stezhko, Yuliya Derbisheva, Lorri Kajenna, Amber Sun, and Silmairel. You are all so gifted.

Thank you to Courtland and Grayson for being my light, my heart, and my soul. Thank you to the most amazing friends and family I could ever ask for. Nana, you rock and I love you more.

Thank you Edmond for being Edmond, and Spirit Lala for bringing the Red Feathered Soul to life.

A very special thank you to Mom, Vivian Marie Brown Baker, for that magical visit and my higher power and all of its angels that brought this message to me to share. Together we can heal.

the Red
Feathered
Soul
...and other Angels in Flight

Chapter One

"Through Darkness Comes Light"

There will come a time in most of our lives when we will encounter such brokenness that we will be faced with two decisions. The first is to walk the rest of our days barely surviving or to turn our pain into purpose. I feel one of our greatest purposes comes in the form of pain and how we can help pull others up from that very same darkness and back into the light.

The story of how the poem "The Red Feathered Soul" came to me was born of that intense pain called grief.

I had lost a brother I adored in 2013. In 2014, I lost a best friend to cancer, and 3 months later, my mother passed away. My husband Jeff and I were unable to have children but filled our life with fur children, our nieces and nephews, and other children that we loved like our own. We rescued Pomeranians and ferrets. They are both natural comedians and they bring joy into our lives daily. During 2013 – 2015, we lost 6 of our fur babies. Basically, in just over 2 years, I lost a great deal of the people and companions I was closest to.

I have learned a few things about life that feel so intrinsically truthful. One of those is that some paths are our destiny. I look back at my life and realize that part of my purpose was to help care for my mother who became very ill while I was in my twenties. I was a caretaker for her along with my sister Sue for the next 20 years. My mother suffered from COPD, renal kidney failure, and dementia in the end. It was a very long and difficult walk home.

My brother who passed away was 17 years older than myself. I adored him. He was so witty and had a child-like personality that made everyone love him. He carried very deep wounds from serving in the Vietnam War. He was a helicopter door gunner and this haunted him his entire life. Wayne passed away from long-term damage from alcohol-induced dementia. His walk home was also very long. Like my mother, I was grieving losing parts of him long before he crossed over.

After my mother passed away, the entire Universe changed in ways I could never imagine. For me, it was the straw that broke the camel's back. Caring for her was so challenging, and in the end with dementia, it was just flat out excruciating and sometimes, completely impossible. While I was so happy for my mother when she was finally free, something happened to me that I couldn't prepare for.

A few days after her passing, I had a panic attack. It was because I couldn't speak to her. You see, once dementia entered into the picture, like many other adult children, I had become her parent. I had a dear friend and talented therapist, Heather Suggs explain to me that this was one of the most unnatural things a child, adult or otherwise, would encounter in life. She was so right. One can never prepare for that role reversal. We never really stop needing our parents.

In her last years, Mom and I usually spoke three times a day even on the days I saw her. For the first time, I realized I could never speak to her again. I had this overwhelming feeling that I needed to make sure she was ok. The silence was deafening. I tried to calm down but to no avail, so I turned to prayer. I prayed that my mother would be sent as a cardinal to let me know she was safe, happy, and free. At that time, I had no knowledge of the cardinal experience. I chose it because I didn't see many and because she wore this really cute cardinal vest. Synchronistically, that vest was the one thing I asked for of hers and I treasure it so much.

Fast forward a couple of days later, I was upstairs putting together her photo boards for her funeral. All of a sudden, I hear my sweet rescue Pomeranian, Luna Bella, barking like crazy downstairs. This was extremely odd because her back legs hardly worked. I had to carry her up and down the stairs. Also, she was a mama's girl and never left my side. I ran downstairs to check on her and there she was barking out the sliding glass door at a cardinal. I was in awe. I dropped to the floor crying, thanking God, the Universe, for this moment. I started talking to mom and the cardinal bounced closer. Our eyes met and it cocked its head in a way that was so comforting. This was the most magical moment in my life. This was the start of more magic to come. Magic that was meant for all of you. Hope, love, and healing.

The next year was a blur. I had to take care of her estate and hopefully, get some closure on this chapter. Our family all needed some peace and to begin that very personal journey of healing. You will find that there are no two people who deal with loss the same way. It comes in waves. There are times you feel completely calm and at one with them, only to wake up craving the ability to speak to them, to hold them the next day. Grief is indeed the most mysterious emotion I have ever yet to encounter. I now just choose to make it like a wave when it hits and flows with it, knowing the tide will shift. During these times, self-care and patience are so important for anyone suffering from loss.

I was on a healing journey – mind, body, and spirit. I set out on a discovery of how to heal, honestly by no choice. My body was tired, my spirit felt starved and my mind had been in fight or flight mode for far too long. I had autoimmune issues and with no choice, I had to slow down. I began to find my way back to the things that brought me joy as a child that I left behind many moons ago. As a child, I was a poet of sorts. I was that kid who would sit and write about trees, animals, seasons, people, and just life in general. Almost a year after my mother passed away, I grabbed a pen and pad of paper and started writing. The words "Red Feathered Soul" came to me. The poem took less than 20 minutes to write, which was how I knew it came from a source. I was just the vehicle and I was meant to share this message, which led to other poems with similar messages.

Red Feathered Soul

When you're lost or feeling down,
Don't despair, just look around.
God made me red so you would see,
I still exist outside your memory.
I make my visits in bright daylight.
You'll hear my song in distant flight.
My cardinal song is a call to you,
To tell you that I miss you too.
I am everywhere and finally free,
Like love you cannot touch or see.
You'll see me in the trees and skies,
I didn't leave, love never dies

- Elle Bee

I also wrote a more personal version of it called "Red Feather Souls". Yes, I should have renamed it to something less like the other title like perhaps "Red Feathered Angels". To be honest, I had no idea if anyone would connect to these poems. I was just doing what I felt called to do.

My pen name, Elle Bee, is actually my initials.

Here is that poem.

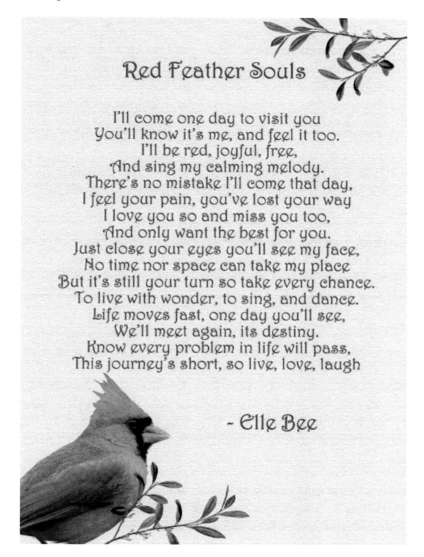

Red Feather Souls

I'll come one day to visit you
You'll know it's me, and feel it too.
I'll be red, joyful, free,
And sing my calming melody.
There's no mistake I'll come that day,
I feel your pain, you've lost your way
I love you so and miss you too,
And only want the best for you.
Just close your eyes you'll see my face,
No time nor space can take my place
But it's still your turn so take every chance.
To live with wonder, to sing, and dance.
Life moves fast, one day you'll see,
We'll meet again, its destiny.
Know every problem in life will pass,
This journey's short, so live, love, laugh

- Elle Bee

I could hear the dearly departed, telling loved ones they left how much they still care and are always thankful for all the love they shared. Still, they want them to live fully, to claim their joy, and to know there is beauty in this life. They want us to know we are still connected and will all be together again, in the most unimaginable state of love we could imagine. A state of no more misunderstandings, only love. There will be no count of wrongdoings. When people leave this dimension, the mind loses that division. All of our needs are met. We LOVE everything and there are no hierarchies of pain. It is just like returning to our innocence. We are safe, we are loved, and we will all be reunited.

After I finished the first "Red Feathered Soul" poem, I knew I was supposed to do something with it. I remember finding this magical artist, jewelry maker/brand named Spirit Lala (yes that is her real name). I fell in love with her artwork and I placed an order just before mom had died. I remembered she had an amazing cardinal piece in her collection. Still, it took me another 6 months after writing the poem to have the courage to ask if they would collaborate with me on a grief gift together to offer in our family gift line. That first gift would be a special design of her breathtaking cardinal necklace, with the "Red Feathered Soul" poem.

I called the first week after New Year. I got a hold of the coolest, wisest man and a kindred spirit named Edmond Bush. He ran her online division and managed the jewelry makers. As I was rambling on nervously about my story, he says, "Lori, oh Lori, I have to interrupt you, you will never guess what I am holding in my hand this very minute. Lori, I have that cardinal piece in my palm." Spirit Lala has a large line of designs. The likelihood of this happening was miraculous. We both stopped because together, we witnessed another sign that this was meant to happen. As he said this, I looked out the window and a cardinal was singing in the tree. I had been listening to some Avett Brothers songs on YouTube, and I looked at my computer and it said "Cardinal Sessions". I was in total awe. This all came from a divine dimension.

Spirit Lala said yes to the collaboration and the next thing we knew, we began selling out of this gift. The entire gift was designed to be a healing experience. I could not believe how well-received they were. I was beyond touched, beyond honored, and beyond grateful.

13

Next, came the other products you asked for.

The greatest gift for me was the customers who shared their stories of angel visits. They kept coming and coming. I finally asked for permission to share these amazing encounters with these angels. Customers began asking for poems about blue jays, butterflies, dragonflies, seagulls, doves, etc. We also have a poem customers love called Angel Signs, because of all the signs people have witnessed. There is this amazing yet soul-crushing experience that happens when our loved ones pass on to another dimension. There really are no words to describe it. Your world stops. It literally stops in a way you could never explain. Suddenly, you feel things you never felt before. Call it energy, call it matter, call it a breeze, but you will feel the spirit surrounding you. Grief is the loneliest part of our journey here, despite the fact that we will almost all experience it. It is just so personal. Of all the elements of nature, I feel grief takes on the form of the ocean. It comes in waves, and sometimes, the waves feel like it will hold you under, that you won't be able to catch your breath. The next day, there is a stillness, a calm, and the feeling that, wow, the Universe, God, a higher power has this and I need not worry. They are with us and will be until we can unite in that mystical dimension they wait for us in. The only thing I am truly certain of is that spirit in its purest form, only wants the very best for us. There is no count of wrongdoings, there are no grudges, only understanding; the knowing that being human can be impossible at times. The love they have for us is unfathomable. Hold on to that. Hold that close to your heart. You will blink and one day, we will all be together again.

The messages that came to me from these poems were clear. They came completely through spirit. Many of the poems demanded that I do not change the message, but only the signs.

I am just beyond grateful to you all for sharing your life with me, for trusting me with your words, your stories, and your beautiful hearts. I hurt for each of you and I have a sacred space with feathers, pennies, crystals, offerings, leaves, shells, etc. This space is for you. I send you all waves of love and healing.

I shared that having children was not a part of my journey here, even though I had wished for them. Please hear me, my dear friends.

We come here, and each and every one of you has such amazing purposes. These purposes come in the form of helping pick someone else up in their time of need. Our pain, when turned to purpose, is the most healing form of medicine ever. I thank you for helping me heal through your amazing stories. I am forever touched.

I am beyond honored that these amazing people shared their life, grief, pain, and hope, not just with me but to help others know - we are not alone. Grab a tissue friends as these stories will be sure to touch your hearts in ways words cannot describe.

Chapter Two

"Cardinals Appear When Angels Are Near"

I would like to start the stories off with one that is very special to me from my amazing nephew and niece John and Monica Baker. John is the son of my brother, Wayne, who passed away. Monica is his daughter-in-law and was very close to Wayne as well. Before I give away their story, I must add that neither of them smokes. This one really got me in the feels because this is so Wayne!

John and Monica Baker from New Baltimore MI shared:

"We have two cardinals that hang out in our backyard. I know one is Wayne. It was really strange too because I was thinking about him the other day when I saw the cardinal and then, John asked me if I smelled cigarette smoke. Every once in a while, we smell it. It only lasts a second or two but I know it's Wayne."

Dawn Allor Godfrey of Clarkston MI shared

"The first anniversary of my mother's death came fast and hard. It was a sad day to remember. A phone call from my dearest friend in the world to wish me love and peace. As we were talking, she looked out her back sliding door, and there, in the trees, was a mama cardinal, and would you believe a baby? Now, neither one of us had ever seen a baby cardinal. But on this day, we both knew immediately what it meant. My mom was letting us know that she found Baby Richard Harold that I had lost in 2019."

Dave Turrel shared:

"My wife died suddenly two months ago. Even though our Christian faith assures me that she is with Christ, I miss her so much. Right after her funeral, I called out to her and a bright red cardinal was flying to the window. That was unusual as it was on a porch with only one opening. It flew out and perched in a tree right over me for quite some time, as I had gone outside. I can't remember when we had seen a cardinal around our home.

A week ago, I was having a tough morning and asked God for strength. I heard a bird singing and turned around on my chair. There was a young cardinal right outside my window singing. It was there for some time, then turned and looked right at my eyes and then flew away."

Marilyn Melancon shared:

"On the day my daddy died, my sister and I were standing outside in the carport. We had thrown some seeds for the birds and along came a bright red male cardinal. He came so close to us, that we were both amazed. When we went into the house, we found that daddy was no longer breathing and had passed away. The next day, Gerald and I went to my dad's house where we were meeting my sisters to go make funeral arrangements. When we pulled into the driveway and got out of the truck, a male and female cardinal landed on the cement just a few feet away from me. That was my sign that my mom and dad were together again."

Brenda Dickhaut of Plessis, New York shared:

"My daughter and I have lived in this house for 21 yrs., not one cardinal ever seen. I have lost most of my family through our 21 years here. I lost my precious daughter on April 6 of this year (2021), the 11th was my 71st birthday. They were awful crying days on the porch with a friend.

My daughter and my SUV were parked at the end of the walk. The first cardinal ever sat on her passenger-side mirror, looked, and then flew away. A smaller one sat on her mirror. One returned with it and I thought that's definitely my Penny, never wanting her mom to be sad. A second cardinal visited a few days later. Her brother was sitting in Penny's kitchen chair by her window, 3 feet from our lilac bush. I was sitting next to my son, we were on the computer and smartphone struggling to find cardinal items, heart easels, and heart urn wreaths for her service. My son nodded to look out Penny's window. Two cardinals were there on the closest branches looking directly at us. My only comfort that day was on the 11th. My son ordered me a two-sided cardinal necklace. One side says "Our love is alive forever." and a cardinal mask for me too. Our love is alive forever here, there, everywhere, and forever— holding me together. Each painful day, I'm one step closer to her."

Deborah Simmons shared:

"My parents passed away in 2017 and 2019. Before my mom passed, she said she would still check in on me and Joe from time to time. We have had cardinals in the yard but this behavior seemed unusual to me. Three days ago, we were awakened by tapping on our bedroom window. Upon further investigation, there was a female and male couple that were trying to

"God made me red so you would see, I still exist outside your memory."

perch on our outside window sill. This went on all day, to the point where we could stand at the window and the only thing separating us was the window pane. This continued throughout the day until dusk. On day two, we were awakened by the gentle taps on our window. By the gentle light of a new day, the female which we have now named Momma was now perched and looking in the window. We have left the windows up overnight and we're blessed with a morning song. We could see the male cardinal which we have named Daddy, in a nearby tree. Again, as the day progressed, the cardinals were perched on the windowsill, sharing the view. Today at dawn, we were given a private concert by Momma & Daddy. I truly believe that my parents are checking in on us. Momma told me that she would look in from time to time. Deep in my heart & soul, I can feel their presence. To God be the Glory."

Vickie Kerr Noble shared:

"A cardinal was waiting for me when I got to work Friday, which was a day off but I ran into the office for a few minutes. My daughter was killed in a car wreck that day on Dec 14th, 2016. For months, I had a red bird that stayed outside my window at work.

Mathew Terronez shared:

"My wife believed in the cardinals so much, I've been awakened many mornings since she passed in January by two cardinals singing in my backyard. Today, after having a bad day, one followed me from the back of the house to the front, sat over me, and sang to me.

Barbara Voss Bass shared:

"Two weeks after my husband of 56 and a half years died from COVID, I was sitting in my family room. I had just returned from my first grief group meeting and was so sad. I was crying uncontrollably. I glanced out my patio window and saw a flash of red. Oh, my dear Lord, a cardinal was in my screened pool enclosure. He had come in through the doggy door. He flew right to me but did not land. He stayed in for about 30 minutes.

Two weeks later, the same thing happened, only this time it was a female cardinal. They both come to see me every day. When I see them, they look at me as if to say I'm here, I'm watching out for you.

No one will ever tell me that is not the spirit of my husband and another family member. Prior to my cardinal experience, I wasn't able to sleep. Now, I sleep all night. God is good."

Cynthia Gosnell shared:

"So comforting! I've been seeing cardinals since my husband passed away suddenly this past February. Lately, a male and a female cardinal have been coming around my front porch.

Your poem is beautiful. So sorry for your losses. I lost my husband of 34 years at the age of 58 suddenly. Did not get to say goodbye. On the day of his death, a cardinal appeared in a tree as I was looking out. I have seen cardinals almost every single day since his death. I can be outside and praying for peace and it seems as if they come from nowhere. The site of a cardinal just gives me so much comfort."

Julie Paysiner shared:

"What a beautiful poem, the words are so heartfelt and loving. I know I see cardinals outside my window off and on and I always say there is David, my husband who has been gone for 2 years. Thank you for posting this."

Cindy Booth Seabright shared:

"What a beautiful poem, thank you for sharing. My Mom passed away 35 years ago, and my sister 2 years ago, who was my rock after mom died. Then last year, my only brother died. I love coming out on my deck and waiting for my cardinals to show up. I knew the saying that says "When Cardinals Appear, Angels are Near". My husband didn't know about it but one day, while he was shopping for flowers for our yard, he came across the most beautiful wind chimes with that saying and cardinals on each chime and surprised me on my birthday with it. It was then that I told him I see cardinals all the time and now he talks to them too."

"*I didn't leave, love never dies.*"

Daniel G. From Michigan shared:

"Last winter, my girlfriend lost her grandma and she said her favorite thing was cardinals. Then whenever I would go outside to smoke, the same one or two cardinals would come to visit me. In winter, with no other birds around. I would tell her I felt like it was her grandmother sending a sign. I honestly did not know this was a thing until recently when people said this about cardinals. There has to be something to this. Just as it's a fact, there's more to life than this. The universe, time, love, our souls, are all endless. How could this be? But yet it is.

Judy Adair Myska of Michigan shared:

"We lost our dear son, Walter, light of our life 7 years ago at the age of 38. Our hearts have been beyond broken.

His angel signs are beyond coincidence and happen frequently, usually as a cardinal but other signs as well.

Recently, my husband and I were on our way to Florida. Driving next to us was the same type of car our son drove and the same color. My husband says to me "I bet Walter's number 33 is on the plate". 33 was his sports number. Sure enough, the car pulls in front of us, and not only is his number 33 on the plate, but there is also a cardinal on it. It brought tears to our eyes. I have no doubt our son surrounds us and will continue to until we can all be reunited together again one day."

Lorraine Gosselin shared:

"My cardinal was singing in my backyard the day before Easter! I looked up and said 'Happy Easter mom!' I was filled with joy!"

"My cardinal song is a call to you, To tell you that I miss you too."

Mary E. Hutchinson-Basmajian shared:

"I'm in tears, as I just lost my mother in March of 2022. She loved red and cardinals. I pray that her spirit is near and she is free to fly with the cardinal. I go out of my house every morning and listen and try to see her. I say hello and good morning to her all the time (cardinals). I was her caregiver as well, she had dementia pretty bad, and that was so hard, her not knowing me or other things. I miss her so much and talking to her and the cardinals is what helps the best."

Gail Latham of Central Falls, North Carolina shared:

"I have found so much peace when they appear. Have you ever been thinking of two people and then two cardinals appear? It's a wonderful experience."

Beth Ann Doulen Miller shared:

"When my beloved brother passed, after his funeral, my mother was reluctantly sitting on the front porch with a neighbor who'd stopped by. She told me 'Beth, a cardinal flew past my face. It was so very close that I could feel its wing against my cheek. Then it flew over to rest on a bush in front of my brother's bedroom window.' I told her 'Mom, it was Danny. He was letting you know he is okay. Everything is okay.' It was a beautiful blessing for her

23

that she needed. They were so close. When she passed, my family and I were climbing a hill while driving on the road. As we crested that hill, a huge flock of cardinals crossed the sky. So much beautiful red color passing over. I acknowledged that it was my mother sending a sign. She knew I'd recognize that she, too, was at peace. I called all the family to tell them because I thought there were so many, it was a message for us all."

Michelle Garrison of Buffalo, New York shared:

"Cardinals hold a special place in my heart. They were my mom's favorite birds. She loved her backyard birds. The summer after my mom passed away, a couple showed up in my backyard. We were able to walk by them no more than a good distance away and they wouldn't fly off. They've been here ever since. I believe they are my mom and dad. They are my favorite birds as well. Some days, they look as though their color is illuminated and they are so bright."

Kimberly Smith of Cox City, Oklahoma shared:

"We were building a house at the lake, very close to where my Grandparents had a cabin when we were growing up. My parents owned our lot and we bought it. We used a lot of repurposed things from my grandparent's farmhouse in building it. All summer, we had 2 male and a female cardinal watching us. My uncle had also passed about 16 years before. They were always there. Two summers ago, a pair built a nest over the top of one of my porch light fixtures. They didn't have eggs in it that year, but they added to it and hatched chicks this year. I think they were messages from my Grandpa, Grandma, and uncle of approval of our lake home."

"We'll meet again, it's destiny."

Margie Siciliano of New York, New York shared:

"When my husband passed on 2 years ago, a male cardinal came and stayed on my picnic table. I ran to get my phone so I could record that moment of sorrow for me but when I returned, it was gone. I've read that they are God's messengers and came to comfort me."

Paula Timpson shared:

"Mom always said she would see a cardinal in spring–a sign her parents were flying to her home for the summer."

Kathy Cunningham of Freedom, Maine shared:

"My mother, who passed away in early January 2014, was an avid bird watcher and typically had 4 or 5 pairs daily at her feeders. My dad passed away in 2005, and she declared that she would starve before she let her birds go hungry; so, the obvious Christmas present from many was huge bags of birdseed. She taught school for many years and instilled the love of cardinals in all of us. We miss her dearly. I had a cardinal tattoo in her honor for my birthday a couple of years ago. My kids said I was too old and would never dare do it, that only made me want it more. My husband gifted it for my 67th birthday."

Brenda Anne DePelsmaeker- Dunlop of Bothwell, Scotland shared:

"Our mom passed away suddenly in 2019. A few days after, we were there together having supper with our dad when a cardinal visited my sister's backyard fence and linger there. My sisters and I cried because we knew mom came to let us know she was happy and safe in heaven."

Michelle Garrison of Buffalo, New York shared:

"The summer after my mom passed away, a cardinal couple began frequenting our backyard. Even though my dad passed away in 1975, I believe that couple is my parents visiting. These birds warm our hearts for a reason."

"When you're lost or feeling down, Don't despair, just look around."

Betty De La Porte shared:

"My aunt had tuberculosis and asked God to give her a sign that she would recover. A red bird (which was not native) appeared on a tree next to her window. She said it was a sign of hope for her. She did recover, got married for 49 years, and she lived to her mid-80s."

Valerie Jeannette Fugazzotto-Rendeiro of Billerica, Massachusetts shared:

*"My resident cardinal came to eat this morning. I've had this pair of
cardinals coming to my yard for quite some time now. They return each year. In the past year, I've discovered why I have these guardians and I know it's my dad and my nana. They've been*

watching over me, since my disappearance over 30 years ago."

Sally Riddell shared:

"The one and only time I saw cardinals in my yard was the day after my son's funeral. That day, a beautiful cardinal flew into my front porch, sat on the wrought iron rail, looked right at me for several minutes, and then flew away. Haven't seen one since. I know it was my son saying "All is well, mom."

Susan Harley-Foltz shared:

"I lost four family members over the past 12 months. Almost daily, cardinals will flap their wings frantically at the side view mirror on the driver's side of my car and the passenger side of my husband's truck; messengers telling me the veil was thinning between life and hereafter for my loved ones."

Sue Dargenio Ciardi shared:

"I lost my 18-year-old son, my only child. It wasn't until a week after he passed, that a red cardinal appeared in our yard. We never had cardinals here before. Now, he's here almost every day. This bird now means so much to me as I know this is my angel boy who watches over his mom and dad."

"This bird now means so much to me as I know this is my angel boy who watches over his mom and dad."

Liz Gettings shared:

"My mom loved all birds but cardinals were her favorite. When she passed, I stayed at my parent's house for a few weeks to keep my dad company. I would sit on the front porch, and every day, a cardinal would come by pretty much at the same time. I am absolutely convinced it was my mom saying hello and keeping me company."

Alice Roth Eppley shared:

"I have Elle Bee's Red feathered Soul poem card framed. It came with a cardinal gift I received after my son passed this past January 2021. I collect cardinals and am blessed to be visited by them almost daily."

JoAnn Rixham shared:

"The cardinal is a strong symbol to me. He came and sang to me the night my mother died. A sign telling me that she had arrived safely in heaven. She has been gone 25 years and I miss her as much now as I did then."

Red Feathered Soul

When you're lost or feeling down,
Don't despair, just look around.
God made me red so you would see,
I still exist outside your memory.
I make my visits in bright daylight,
You'll hear my song in distant flight.
My cardinal song is a call to you,
To tell you that I miss you too.
I am everywhere and finally free,
Like love you cannot touch or see.
You'll see me in the trees and skies,
I didn't leave, love never dies.

- Elle Bee

Sheila Lynn Horn Kaplan shared:

"My husband of 53 years passed away this March 2021 from COVID. In April, my son found this beautiful little Cardinal sitting outside his window."

Jill Webb shared:

"My father-in-law passed away about 3 am in Oct 2019. About 7 am I went outside to walk the dogs. A bright red cardinal basically dive-bombed me, rested on a trellis in their yard, and stared at me for about 30 seconds before flying off. I knew it was him wanting me to tell our family everything was okay for him. I bursted into tears and rushed in to tell what had happened. Much to my surprise, none of them had ever heard about cardinal angels. This convinced me more that it was my dad."

Toni Tomassoni Barnes shared:

"A short time after my husband passed, I was sitting in my living room looking out the window when a cardinal landed on a branch next to the window. Later the same day, my mom came to visit. Again, the cardinal appeared in the same place. A week or so later, a storm damaged the tree and it was cut down. After that, I was sitting on my back steps and I noticed a cardinal sitting on an electrical box a few feet from me facing the other way. I said 'Russ, if that's you turn around.' It turned around and flew away. I haven't seen any cardinals since."

Lisa Hilton Pendreigh of London, Ontario shared:

"Outside my mom's window at the nursing home every morning, the cardinals would sing up a storm. In the morning she passed, again they were singing, I lay beside her and said 'Dad's calling you, mom. It's okay. Go be with him.' She took her last breath."

Michele Jordan Colburn of Roswell, Georgia shared this beautiful story of how her saving an injured cardinal, changed her perspective in life:

"One day, I got up from a very restless night. I had not slept well and had a lot on my mind and on my heart. I took Mason to school. I was pulling down my street when I noticed this little guy on the road. I pulled to the side of him thinking he would fly away as my car approached. As I went by, I noticed he did not move. I looked in my side view and he was still there. I pulled my car over and started walking towards him. As I walked towards him, I expected him to either fly or at least start struggling to get away. He did not move. I walked straight to him and picked him up. He never attempted to struggle away from me. I did not have to restrain him at all. I examined him and saw no sign of injury. Yet, I knew something was not right. I pulled him close to my heart and began to gently pet him. I decided I would take him to the CNC. They help a lot of wildlife. It would be a couple of hours before they opened. As I continued to hold him, there was an immediate bond. He would look me right in the eye and put his beak to my nose.

I was finally able to take him to CNC. Unfortunately for this little guy, they do not take songbirds. Only birds of prey. However, they were kind enough to examine him. Upon examination, they were able to determine he had broken his clavicle. They told me just like humans, it is very painful for the birds. The thought is he was hit by a car. They recommended a place to take him. It is located in Decatur, which was going to take a little over an hour one way with traffic.

I had a full day and did not know how I could do it. As I sat in the car trying to decide what I was going to do, he sang. I stopped my thought process and looked down at him. He was looking at me from the little box I had him in. As I continued to look at him, he let out a couple of more little notes. Tears began to fill my eyes. This tiny little creature was in pain with a broken clavicle, and yet, he still sang. I sat there for a few minutes just looking at him. I reached over and gave him a gentle stroke on his head and said 'Thank you, little guy.'

"Thank you, little guy."

I called Seth and asked him to reschedule all of my meetings for the day. I called the songbird place and a wonderful human by the name of Nancy told me to bring him in. I took off to Decatur. When we arrived, Nancy examined him and confirmed he had a broken clavicle but that his air sacs were full as well and needed to be released. She explained to me the process and told me he had a three to four-week recovery ahead. She let me know that some make it and some do not because of the uncertainty of what he may have going on internally due to being hit. She also informed me that if he did make it, then at the end of his recovery, he would need to be released where I found him. Cardinals generally have a family. He has had a rough road. There were a couple of times she wasn't sure he was going to make it, as he stopped eating a few times. He pushed through.

I was able to pick him up on Monday to release him back into nature. I share this experience with you because this little bird reminded me that we can still sing even when we are struggling. When we are struggling and in pain, we can still make a difference. He reminded me that every living thing is significant, no matter what. If it has life, it deserves love. It is a birthright!

He reminded me to stop, take it slow, and always, ALWAYS, let *love lead. On a day when I was struggling with some pretty heavy things, he reminded me to sing."*

Nancy Casella Morton of Waltham, Massachusetts shared:

"My dad passed away in December after battling Vascular Dementia which is a horrible disease. A few weeks after he went to heaven, my mom, sister, and myself were sitting around the dining room table, looking to get the final details done for my dad's headstone when something caught my eye. As I looked up, sitting in a tree with the snow coming down was the most beautiful red cardinal I have ever seen staring right at me. He seemed to be glowing in red! At that very time, we were discussing whether my dad liked loons or cardinals better and I guess we had our answer. I know that when God sends a cardinal, it's a visitor from heaven and that when cardinals appear, angels are near. The three of us could feel his presence. It was the most amazing thing ever and I got to share it with my mom and sister. My younger brother said that he has seen a cardinal in his backyard every day when he goes home for lunch, one that he had never seen before. I guess he is checking up on all of us. Thanks for the visit dad. We all miss you so very much.

"Just close your eyes you'll see my face,
No time nor space can take my place."

Diane Pina shared:

"Today is July 1st, 1 month that my dog Ruby passed. Unbelievably, a red cardinal came to visit today, he actually pecked in the window until I looked. I am so excited that after reading everybody's posts online, I am a true believer that my dog, Ruby, is telling me that she is happy and not suffering anymore."

Judy Blevins shared:

"I have a wonderful friend. Her name is Sharon. No, we do not see each other very often. We don't live next door to each other. But our hearts and minds have connected. She seems to know when I need a 'pick me up' and I know when she needs it too. We will all of a sudden send a little note or picture or a music box or a wind chime. We both love the cardinal. She has a beautiful granddaughter in heaven that comes to visit her daily, and I have my mama visiting daily here. I have been very low, probably at my lowest two times here lately. She sends me a message telling me that there is something on its way. I cry. Not because of my sadness but because my heart has talked to her and she has responded to me with a gift of a cardinal. Thank you, God, for sending me this friend. But I believe my mama is in heaven rocking beautiful Aspyn. The two have gotten together and put us together."

Abbi Czerwiec of Westfield, Massachusetts shared:

"I lost my Babci in April. A cardinal always came to visit her and we knew it was my Dziadek stopping by to say hi. After she passed, a male and female cardinal visited my aunt every day. For Christmas, I made my aunt a cardinal lantern. It's a way to remember that my Babci is never too far away."

Candy Baker of Sidney, Ohio shared:

"I too lost my mother almost 3 years ago. Although her leaving was quick, it left a hole in my heart. I live several 100 miles away and even though I made it there before she passed, she was unresponsive when I arrived. I always felt the need to hear her again one last time. But in the dark months after, I was visited by my red feathered friend. Very comforting and still today, I see my red feathered friends whenever I'm down or sad. Certainly, a message from mom telling me she's okay and I am too."

Carla Watts of Statesville, North Carolina shared:

"I lost my precious momma on December 14, 2020. It's been a long hard year. I lost my dad on February 15, 1985. One Saturday, I stepped out on my porch, and there, they were together. The tears flowed but I talked to them and I felt that they were listening. When I was done, I thanked them for checking on me and told them how much I loved and missed them both. In an instant, they were gone. But I know they will be back. As bright and beautiful as ever."

Colleen Sullivan Howard of Jefferson, Georgia shared:

"Back in 2017, my oldest brother was diagnosed with lung cancer. I worked from home and I heard this bird singing in my backyard. I got up and scanned the fence line and there he was, the first time I ever saw a bright red cardinal. Everyday for the next year, Red sat out on the fence everyday singing. In July of 2018, my brother moved to a hospice in Florida and as my sister and I sat in his room with him, I heard a song that was so familiar. But it couldn't be Red, he was in Georgia at my house. I opened the shutter in his room and there he was, a Red hanging on the soul feeder singing. That was Wednesday, July 11 (my sister's birthday). We both started to cry. Red came by for the next 2 days and when my brother took his last breath, Red was sitting on the ledge at the bottom of the window. My sister and I knew my mom and dad came to take our brother home with them. In 2019, we moved to our new house in North GA, and I was working in my new home office and to my surprise, I heard that oh, so familiar song and looked up and there he was, my Big Red found me again. I know during my happy and sad times, my Big Red is always there."

"I know during my happy and sad times, my Big Red is always there."

Marie Taylor of Gonzales, Louisiana shared:

"Whenever I see a cardinal, I know it is my grandson, Wayne, telling me 'MawMaw, I am alright I am with Jesus.' It makes my day but also brings on the tears."

Sarah Mendes of Tulare, California shared:

"My step dad passed away in a car accident driving home to California from Arkansas. The accident happened in Amarillo, Texas on I-40. My mom, sister, and I flew out to Texas and picked up his ashes then flew to Arkansas to have a service for him with his family who are all in Arkansas. I wanted to go to our childhood home in Arkansas so when we got there, we did. Sadly, our house was demolished and a new frame was being built. We walked around the area of our old home and on the side of where our

house once sat, there was a red cardinal in the bushes. I instantly thought of my stepdad. Like he knew we would be going by there, so he made his way over. I tried to record it in the trees but I was so in awe over this cardinal, I didn't even record where the bird was and only got a glimpse of it in my video. I was so sad. But anyways, when I was recording it and as I tried to get a little closer, it flew right past my head, and then it was gone. I will always feel that was my stepdad letting us know he was there with us and he is ok."

Deborah Hudak-Caballero of Hazlet, New Jersey shared stories of her several encounters with the red feathered friend:

"My dad passed away in July 2014. That's when I saw my first red cardinal. Then my son-in-law passed in October 2014, three months after my dad. And a second red cardinal came. (My grandson was only 10 months old, that was his dad). Then in 2019, my mom passed away and a female cardinal started coming around. It's amazing that they all showed up when they did! My grandson finds comfort in the red cardinal as I do. We've been in 3 different states for vacation this year and a cardinal has shown up everywhere we went. If I'm having a bad day, a red cardinal shows up and I know I'm going to be alright! We went a little crazy with the red cardinal for Christmas this year."

"The other day, I had to send an important email that was regarding my future. As soon as I hit send, a red cardinal landed on the bird feeder right out my kitchen window. I said, 'There is dad.' Everything is going to go okay."

"I brought a beautiful cardinal lantern at Hobby Lobby for my grandson. He is 7 and lost his dad when he was just 9 months old. He loves red cardinals and sees them as a sign his daddy is around."

Lorraine Kiskiel-Massey Negron of Fair Lawn, New Jersey shared:

"My 41-year-old son died suddenly from a massive heart attack. All summer long, a cardinal was here. I knew it was him. It helped me get by in some sort of way. But life for me will never be the same as it is for many when they lose a loved one."

Terrie Bray Marlowe of Sebastian, Florida shared:

"A cardinal sat outside my mom's window at the hospice house, the day mom passed. I told her it was Art (my step-dad) waiting to show her the way to her heavenly home. Her time was close, so I told her it was okay to go whenever she was ready. She passed soon after that. The nurse and aide told me they had never seen a cardinal outside any of the windows before that day, so we believe it was her angel waiting to show her the way home. I see cardinals quite often and tell mom, thank you for the sign that you are ok."

Janice Kelly of Fayetteville, Arkansas shared:

"I lost my brother this year. As I was sitting on my porch visiting with my sister, a cardinal flew right in front of me and sat in a

small peach tree. I remarked, "Hello, brother. Been waiting for you to drop by". He sat in that little tree until I explained the story to my sister then flew away."

"I see cardinals quite often and tell mom thank you for the sign that you are ok."

Susan Koenig Argott of Belvidere, New Jersey shared:

"My son and his family received a cardinal ornament with the Red Feathered Soul poem by Elle Bee attached. My husband passed away in April of this year. As my son was walking towards the tree, the lights flickered. I was in the bathroom and the lights flicked in there, too. When I read the poem, they flickered near me. Nowhere else in the house. Only around my son and me. It gave me so much comfort. I know it was my husband. The holidays are difficult and filled with sadness since. This brought some joy into my heart."

Red Feathered Soul

When you're lost or feeling down,
Don't despair, just look around.
God made me red so you would see,
I still exist outside your memory.
I make my visits in bright daylight,
You'll hear my song in distant flight.
My cardinal song is a call to you,
To tell you that I miss you too.
I am everywhere and finally free,
Like love you cannot touch or see.
You'll see me in the trees and skies,
I didn't leave, love never dies.

- Elle Bee

Debbie Stahl Foley of Richmond, Michigan shared:

"My mother passed away 12 years ago this Christmas and my father passed on April 28th this year 2021. He lived in Florida and I was down there for the last six weeks taking care of him and his dog, Candy. The day after he passed, I took Candy to the dog park. It was early evening and no one else was there. I was sitting on a chair and across the way from me, two cardinals flew out of trees and landed on the chair directly in front of me. They sat there and looked directly at me. Tears were pouring down as I said "Hello, mom and dad!" I am glad to see you are together again. They sat

there looking at me for a few more minutes and then flew away together. It brought me such peace."

Kevin Cockrum of Cleveland, Texas shared:

"In September 2021, I lost my mother to COVID-19. Four days later, my little brother passed away at age 32 from the same virus. I was having a really sad, hard day as Thanksgiving was approaching. I am a firm believer that when you see a cardinal that it's an angel of a loved one. My husband comes in to show me two pictures he has taken and he happened to see two different ones. I knew then we weren't alone on Thanksgiving and they were watching my family, and my brother and his family, and my brother was watching over his kids."

"I'll be red, joyful, free, And sing my calming melody."

Chelsea Sink of Tucson, Arizona shared:

"Thank you all so much for sharing the love for cardinals with me. They're very special to me. I've lost so many loved ones and when I look out my window and see my birdfeeder with cardinals eating around it, I know they are with me in spirit and I'm filled with joy and comfort."

Catherine Cas Shadis of Euless, Texas shared:

"I am having a cardinal yule this year. I've lost so many that I loved dearly. My younger brother passed this March and we, his siblings, feel his loss so much right now. Love when the cardinals visit my feeders."

Tina Wack of Lynchburg, Virginia shared:

"My cousin that was really close to me passed away and I didn't get to say goodbye. As I was just sitting and thinking about her, all of a sudden, my daughter and I heard a big thump and we went outside on my porch and found a cardinal on my table. We thought he was hurt but he wasn't. He flew from my hand to my daughter's hand. He was so beautiful and so I took a picture and felt like my cousin was here with me and as I felt relief, he then flew away"

Linda McKenna shared:

"My husband Jim lost his father in 2004, and the two of them were so close. So much alike and genuine a gentleman. It broke my husband with his loss. We were at the hospital at the hospice all day. We came home around 2:45 am and tried to go to bed. Within minutes, the phone rang and yes, we were going back to the hospital. We had an evergreen tree outside our bedroom window and a cardinal was in the tree, looking at us and singing. We got there in time for goodbyes.

Every holiday, for years, there is a visit from his father (through a cardinal) to our house. On top of that, Jim could whistle exactly like the cardinal! Beyond belief that they would have conversations through whistling every time. I lost my sweet loving husband, Jim in 2014 and I have been blessed to have visits from the cardinal. I love it as I know it's Jim! Of course, I can't whistle close to Jim. But the cardinal still sings back to me. Thank you for the chance to share this with you. Love remains forever!"

Carol Wonderly shared:

"I have been blessed to have a male and female cardinal come and be in my big round flower bed every year. Sometimes, they come next to the tree next to the house and sing to me. I always talk back to them. I always say they are there in place of my husband, parents, in-laws, and grandparents. So many are watching over me and my family. I love them so much."

Cardinals
APPEAR WHEN
Angels
ARE NEAR

Diane Godwin shared:

"I lost my best friend after 35 years of friendship. After the funeral, I came home and was sitting on my deck crying at the thought of her loss. All of a sudden, I looked up, and on my deck rail was a beautiful red cardinal. I had a big sense of inner peace that she was no longer suffering but in a much better place. I have several cardinals that visit me daily. I talk to them and thank them for the sense of inner peace they provide me. Yes, cardinals are angels."

Sandy Shattuck of Saint Louis, Michigan shared:

"My mother passed away almost two years ago. It made the holidays very difficult, to say the least. We were eating our Christmas dinner when my daughter called me to the window. In my car was a female cardinal. She stayed for 30 minutes just hopping around on top of my car. It was so beautiful."

Jennifer Russell of Elmira, New York shared:

"My mom died in 2020. She always loved cardinals. I even bought her at one time, a cardinal doormat. After she had passed, my husband and I were sitting in the backyard. What was flying in the yard and sitting on the fence post was a beautiful red cardinal. We both said 'There's mom, watching us.' It was a crying but beautiful moment. Love you, mom."

Betty Snow of Fort Madison, Iowa shared:

"I had just come home from the hospital where my husband had

just passed away. I pulled into the drive and looked over at our willow tree. There sat a beautiful red cardinal and I knew my husband was in good hands. I have collected cardinal items ever since."

Mary Stewart shared:

"I was so overwhelmed with problems and every time I prayed, things got worse. I was well into losing my faith that there was even a God. So I prayed and asked God to send a red bird if he was real. All day long, I waited and watched, No red bird. As I got ready for bed, I opened a drawer and there was a birthday card I had received earlier with a beautiful red bird on it. I said to God 'Not a paper one.' Faith is somewhat renewed. May have to pray and ask again as caretaking days take a real emotional toll on a person."

Diane L. Patterson shared:

"My daughter bought me a cardinal wind chime from Amazon and the Red Feathered Soul poem by Elle Bee was with it. She bought it three weeks after my husband died from a terrible accident. I read it everyday. She told me "Mom, I bought you a little present. I hope you like it." I love it. So, I have the poem in a frame in my kitchen. I am constantly looking for birds in the morning and listening to the wind chime when I can. Thank you, Sarah. I love both the poem and the cardinal wind chime. And thank you, Elle Bee."

Karen E Lee of Hermitage, Tennessee shared:

"My mother passed away 10 years ago today. Growing up, I remember her love for red birds as she and my grandmother affectionately called them. Anyway, after my mom passed, I prayed all the time for her to give me a sign that she was okay. Fast forward to Mother's Day 2012, I went into my kitchen and opened the curtains on the kitchen window like I do every day. Outside the window, sitting on the hood of my car was a red bird that I swear to this day was looking right at me. It was at that time I knew my mom was okay. I've continued to see them over the years and they always give me comfort."

Jeanmarie Badaracco shared:

"This is so beautiful. I understand what it means completely. My mom has always loved cardinals. And I love them, too. When I am sad or upset, a cardinal will show up. God sent my mom to me as a cardinal to make me feel better."

Marcia Hartzler shared:

"My husband passed away on Christmas morning. The next day, as we were sitting at the kitchen table making plans, my grandson came in and said 'Grandma, Grandpa is here.' We couldn't understand what he meant. He said, 'Look out the window.' And there was a cardinal looking in. Grandpa was a cardinal fan."

"It was at that time I knew my mom was okay."

Ann May of Shenandoah, Virginia shared:

"In 2015, l lost two of my very best friends within three months. My Mama in September 2015 and then my dad in December 2015. I was so close to my parents. They were my world. I lived right beside them all my life. When daddy got sick and could not do things outside, I would always help. When I would shovel snow, he would get upset and send Mama to the door to tell me to stop shoveling and get in the warm house. That first winter without them, we had a huge snowstorm. I was out shoveling and I heard this sound. I looked up on the telephone line and it was a red cardinal and he was really, really making lots of noise. It was my

Mama saying 'Your daddy said quit shoveling and get in this warm house.' The bird followed me all the way across the sidewalk until I stopped and went inside. They are still looking after me."

"This journey's short, so live, love, laugh."

Mary Seager shared:

"My youngest son lived with me for a while. When it was rainy, I would sit on my side porch and listen to cardinals. I would watch the cardinals from my kitchen window and call my grandchildren over, so they could see this beautiful bird I loved so much. I lost my son in August 2021. A little while after he passed, we had a gentle rain and I sat out on the side porch to listen. A cardinal appeared and sang his sweet song, back and forth from the fence to the bird feeder in rain, he sang!"

Joyce Neale of Montreal, Quebec shared:

"My most amazing sight of the cardinals was at Easter. We had the entire family in the yard. We saw a momma, daddy, and three baby cardinals. I am sure it was their initial flight. My dear, Cory, sent them to us."

Beverly Clawson Trivette of Poga, Tennessee shared:

"My mom passed away in May 2017. I feel like a part of me passed away when she did. I didn't understand the meaning of cardinals at that time but she loved to feed the birds and she liked to watch them. Then I found out the meaning, so I started feeding them, and right away, I started seeing cardinals. I would go outside to see them and just smile and say 'I love you, mom.' Your poem is absolutely beautiful, Elle Bee."

Dottie Hegedus Feisel of Mountain Top, Pennsylvania shared:

"I lost my sister two years ago and I miss her so much. The cardinals come every day to our deck a few weeks after her death. They used to actually fly over my head on my deck swing, so close I could feel them."

Phyllis Godsey shared:

"My son was gone for about a year when the most beautiful red bird kept coming to the back yard flying around. But one day, it flew all the way up into the covered porch with only one way in and out. I was standing at the door in awe of everything I was seeing! All I could think about was my son, Shawn and I started to cry. I miss him so much!"

Mary M. Andersen shared:

"I have loved cardinals all my life. They are beautiful birds and bring me a sense of peace every time I see one. I lost my beloved husband in 2001 and every time I see a cardinal outside in my tree, I feel his presence and am so grateful for the feeling. I've lost many family members over the years and always look for a cardinal whenever I miss them."

"You'll see me in the trees and skies, I didn't leave, love never dies."

Eileen Boudreau of Lady Lake, Florida shared:

"The Red Feathered Soul poem card by Elle Bee is so special and beautiful. My daughter loves cardinals. Her dad who passed away was a lover of them, too. Every time we see one, we know he has come to say hello."

" I know they are giving my loved ones and I time together again."

Sara Smith shared:

"I'm a firm believer in angels and cardinals. We have three that come to visit us each winter. I really miss my parents and grandma during the holidays. Each of them loved cardinals. One sits on the clothesline, another sits on the yard swing, while the other sits on the grill. I know they are giving my loved ones and me time together again."

Rhonda Copeland Capps shared:

"All the cardinal stories are beautiful and true. My brother died suddenly in February 2021. I have a cardinal that visits me everyday."

Paula Gangemi of Erie, Pennsylvania shared:

"Today is four years since I lost my baby brother, he was 55. When I opened my door one morning, a beautiful cardinal was singing from a nearby bush. I truly believe my brother sent him to remind me of his love, and that he watches over me. I pray that others receive the same comfort from these heavenly messengers. Gods' Blessings."

Mary McLemore of Monroe, North Carolina shared:

"I love when cardinals come to my feeders. I know in my heart that it is from my husband and my mom."

Dede Harrill of Madisonville, Tennessee shared:

"My husband of 54 years passed away in 2020. This past summer, a pair of cardinals built a nest on my back porch. This was right across from the French window of my dining room. I could also see them from my living room. There is a wooden swing hanging right beneath the heavy-duty board, built by my husband that will seat three comfortably. The birds were not afraid of anyone sitting and swinging beneath the nest. Or the Rottweiler who likes to lay on the back porch. Friends and Family enjoyed seeing and hearing the cardinals. I'm hoping they return in the spring."

Rene Parsons Howard shared:

"I have been looking for and seeing cardinals since my son passed away last year. I count them too. I often see eight of them at once. One day, I saw ten. After thinking about it, I realized that we have lost ten people in our families over the years. I know for sure that the biggest one represents my son. I see them all the time."

Allie Hamilton shared:

"My daddy passed away in February 2019 and I have this one particular cardinal that has been around since then and he always looks in my kitchen window at me for long periods of time. I started calling him daddy."

Eileen Mahan of Pelzer, South Carolina shared:

"My very dearest friend and I had many cardinal experiences. We would drive around our area of rural upstate South Carolina and so many times, we see two cardinals flying beside us or on a tree

or fence. We knew it was our dads who we both lost at young ages. We miss them so much! It was just one of many special moments we shared just the two of us. Lesley's health became worrisome in October of 2020. She turned 48 and seemed to suddenly have various health problems. In 2021, we prayed for answers and a return to health so we could get back to our fun adventures. She had many difficulties and stresses, but she remained optimistic. By late summer, her health rapidly declined. Three hospitalizations over two months led her to hospice care the 3rd week of October. Unfortunately, she passed away a week later. Her death has left enormous emptiness in my life and I cannot believe that I have to go on every day without her. Lesley loved our Lord and her death was a true blessing for her. I am grieving this loss and looking for our cardinal angels. She is healed, whole, and beautiful! I know I will join her in Heaven when God calls me home."

Karen Johnston of Snellville, Georgia shared:

"Whenever I see a cardinal, I know it's my daughter Kristin saying 'I love you' and 'I'm at peace."

"I love you and I'm at peace."

Amber Hughes Del Giudice shared:

"Our oldest daughter passed away unexpectedly in January 2021, which was also her 15th birthday. My dad also passed away in July 2021. This will explain everything.

This year has been anything but ordinary for our family. I honestly thought the holidays would be a very difficult time for all of us. I was dreading them at the beginning of the year and I'm not going to say they are easy by any means. We've grown closer as a family and found wonderful ways to honor our sweet Alexis. This has made the grieving process a bit easier for each of us. We made a 'Memorial Tree' that is located in Alexis's bedroom. We were given this by our sweet friends. We've decided to leave it up year round and decorate it for the different holidays. The first holiday we decided to start with is Christmas. We always put up our tree and decorations the weekend after Thanksgiving. Well, we made an exception one night and broke the rule. Aryana (our youngest daughter) really wanted to decorate it. To see her excitement for Christmas and to honor Alexis there, was no way at all I was saying no.

It came out absolutely beautiful and I enjoyed decorating it with her. We're so blessed to have been gifted most of the ornaments for the tree from many of our family and friends. The red lights were my dad's as that was his favorite color, and of course, the red for the cardinals. Also, the Santa that is climbing the ladder was my dad's too. Aryana insisted on using it next to Alexis's Tree to remember Papaw too."

Shirley Sam McGann Corrigan of Triangle, Virginia shared:

"I store my bird seed in an old metal trash can that was my dads from long ago. I went out and cleaned some snow off the grass, filled the feeder pan and the lighthouse feeder, and sprinkled some feed on the ground. The next day, the birds just kept coming. Looked out and there was a momma and daddy cardinal. I chalk it up to it being my mom and dad who came to visit. My mom has been gone 18 years and my dad will be 6 years a month after."

Tania Luna shared:

> *"I dedicated a Christmas tree I dressed with four cardinals to mom and dad to represent my family. I'm also a bird watcher. I always say to my four kiddos 'when you see a cardinal, dad and I are always there. So when you see one, be happy, your mom and dad came to visit. We are alive of course. But my grandmother will always tell me that. I always say "find me in your dreams where I will always remain"*

Linda Day shared:

> *"9 months ago today, Lonnie, my husband went to his forever home. This morning, I woke to the cardinal song. The same night, I saw the 'Red Feathered Soul' poem card of Elle Bee. Just the heartfelt I needed to see because I watch for the cardinal birds each day."*

> *"I am everywhere and finally free, Like love you cannot touch or see."*

Sherrie Griggs Shell shared:

> *"I lost my husband, suddenly, 12-26-20. My Red visits most days at lunchtime. He sits and just looks in the window. I know he's my Angel. He comforts me so much. I visit the cemetery often and he appears there showing off his wonderful singing voice. God Bless You."*

Shirley Lewis Sizemore of Fruitvale, Texas shared:

"I never had any cardinals at my house until after my mom passed away. My mother was a bird lover and had bird feeders everywhere. Her bird feeders always had cardinals but mine have not. But after she passed away, I started to see cardinals almost daily. Mama had sent her birds to my house to let me know she was watching over us."

Bonnie Orfin of Warren, Ohio shared:

"When my husband died, my son wanted me to spend the night at his house. I was sitting at the kitchen table and asked him to put a chair by the window to see if there were any cardinals outside. After he did that and my back was turned to sit down, he screamed, "Mom, look on the fence." There sat two cardinals. I think the whole town heard me scream and cry."

Peggy Seppala Dever of Austin, Texas shared:

"We lost our mother before Christmas in 2019. I was very lost after her passing. I was with my folks at that time. After I moved to Texas to be near my son, my patio faces a ravine and this red feathered friend would come every day and I would feed him. I told my sister about it and she also had one in her yard. I looked up what it meant and it said a loved one. Winter came and went. Now, he had his mate and two little ones and I kept feeding them. He would feed his little ones. It was so cool. They were never afraid of me."

Sheila Lescord of Bellows Falls, Vermont shared:

"I have cardinal visitors from time to time and it's very comforting to me. When my mom passed, my daughter and I were in the room holding on to my mom's hands when something hit the window. We looked towards the window and there sat a cardinal. It gave us such comfort to be able to think that my mom was released from suffering. My daughter and I believe!"

Floyd Walters of Barberton, Ohio shared:

"We lost my sister a few months ago from COVID-19. After the funeral, and about a couple of weeks ago, there was a red cardinal, on our railing on the front porch. We are always looking for them to come back every day ever since, especially when it's nice outside."

Sending you waves of
love,

peace,

and healing.

Nancy Hatton of Stonewall, Oklahoma shared:

"I understand the pain everyone is going through, too. I was a caregiver to my poppa, mom, dad, and husband. I miss them everyday and long to tell them that I love and miss them. I have cardinals in my yard all of the time. They are the most beautiful birds to me."

Bonnie Fowler of Turnersville, New Jersey shared:

"I've always had a birdfeeder and loved it in particular when the cardinals came around. Two days after my husband died, a white cardinal, red tufted only came and looked in my den window. I firmly believe that it was him saying 'I'm in heaven and all's well.' I never saw a white cardinal before and I haven't seen one after."

Kathy Beasley Schmuker of Alvarado, Texas shared:

"My husband passed September of 2021 and upon returning from his funeral, there was a cardinal perched on our back deck railing, waiting for me to get home. I usually see him daily. I talk to them as I would my husband. They truly listen."

Lisa Brotzman Mckerchie shared:

"A few days after my father passed, I stood by my back slider doors, not sure of what I was looking for. I was grieving very hard. Tears would not stop. All of a sudden, a cardinal landed in the pine tree right off my deck. It stayed there for hours. I could not take my eyes off it. My tears turned to a warm smile. I had my peace."

"My tears turned to a warm smile. I had my peace."

60

Sandra Blair-Kasch of Indianapolis, Indiana shared:

"My dad just passed away in December 2021 and I had a spiritual experience in my tears of sadness. I was blessed with a flock of cardinals that day."

Garey Chambers of Opelika, Alabama shared:

"Only God would have come up with this idea to let us know we still have our loved ones with us. You always see this red cardinal shortly after losing someone close to you. Plus, what bird could be any prettier to remind you of that very special person who is now in heaven with Jesus? God is so wonderful!"

Melda Noe shared:

"My daughter passed away in December of 2020. She was brain dead, so we decided to let her fly home with the angels. The very next morning, I went to the front window and pulled my curtains open. There on my front gate was a red cardinal sitting and staring at me. I knew it was a sign from my daughter, telling me she was ok. The cardinal sat there for a while, just watching me. I believe with everything in me, that was my daughter."

Denise Schevikhoven of Napoleonville, Louisiana shared:

"I can relate to everyone's story. My husband and I have a 7-year-old son together. In April 2021, he was diagnosed with lung cancer. In July 2021, he went to heaven. We all had COVID and he also was just starting week-3 of Cancer treatments. It was so hard for me and my son; we didn't even get to say goodbye."

"I make my visits in bright daylight,
You'll hear my my song in distant flight."

Pamela Lynn Roark shared:

"I appreciate the stories of when a cardinal comes to visit after a loved one has passed. That is how I got started feeding my birds. I lost five family members within two years and moved in with my mother to take care of her. I was having my coffee one morning out on our porch and in our little tree were five cardinals bright and beautiful in the morning sun. It did give me a sign that my family was alright and sending their love."

Kathleen Iliff of Warrenton, Virginia shared:

"Ever since my son passed away three years ago in April, cardinals have surrounded me. It's so amazing. Just today, they gathered in the pine trees outside my bedroom window and responded when I talked to them. They are a wonderful blessing and I thank God everyday."

Jo Powell Bruenning of Anderson, South Carolina shared:

"One day, I lost my gold necklace with a cross my son brought me years ago. I never took it off. I just lost it and we looked everywhere, tore the house apart and outside too. Never found it. Today, I went out to feed my cardinals and I saw one on the ground. I believe a stray cat got him. It upset me so much. I buried him in the backyard. I did my verse of the day and

prayed. I went outside to pray for the cardinal where I buried him. I came back into my bedroom and something caught my eye, beside my bed, there laid my gold cross! I was in complete shock! Y'all I cried and cried. I have said for a month all I wanted to find was the cross. And there it was! I got on my knees thank God and I looked up and there was a cardinal in my apple tree looking at me. ⸢OBJ⸣It was a female."

Ann Weintraut of Atlanta, Georgia shared:

"Yesterday would have been my grandson's birthday. He passed away almost two years ago. My daughter wanted to do a balloon release to celebrate his birthday. While waiting for her to bring the balloons over, my daughter-in-law spotted a cardinal up in the tree. It was such

Karen Harrison shared:

"WOW, that is beautiful. God sent me the cardinals to ease my pain and to let me know my Son was okay. My Son was run over by a tractor trailer while walking. I thought I was going to lose my mind, I felt I failed him. I wasn't there when he died. In the blink of an eye he was gone. He had lived with me for 25 years. I was lost. One day I was sitting on my front porch and suddenly there was a red cardinal sitting on my fence. It was staring at me as I began to smile and talk to my son. It was like he was letting me know that he was okay, free of sickness, and happy. Every morning I would rush outside to see the red cardinal. I found peace as I talked to the bird. I thanked God every time I saw the beautiful bird. In one year, we lost our nephew, my son, my mother-in-law, then my dad and mom just 19 days later. A couple of months later there were three cardinals on my fence and I cried as I said hello Mom, Dad and Michael. I now feed the birds and enjoy seeing the cardinals daily. A touching moment knowing he came to celebrate with us."

**Patricia Davidson Shirah of Colorado Springs, Colorado shared this
beautiful poem:**

"Redbirds from Heaven"

*Oh, mama, was that you that I saw just today...
in the eyes of those Redbirds as they flew away?
For I've never seen so many gathered in one place,
like they were waiting just for me
with your own Heaven-sent embrace!
I felt it too as I looked up
surprised at the Sight,
of all those pretty red Birds dancing 'round me in their flight!
They came from out of nowhere,
those red beauties I know you loved,
what better way to send your feelings
from way up there above!
I felt it go right through me--
as they circled me, I knew-,
that such a good warm feeling
could come from only you!
It felt so strong, that I found myself calling out your name...
just to open up my eyes to see
your Redbirds play their games.
as fast as they came-
they were gone again...
I know now they can't stay,
They've delivered their message to me from you,
but I'll still watch for them everyday!
Cause I know now that was you today...
with your little surprise!
Oh mama ,
I saw you today
--- in those RedBirds eyes!
'86*

Cathy Barton McCaig shared:

"The anniversary of my parents' death is in March. My dad passed in 2015, and my mom in 2017, both from complications from Alzheimer's. It brings me comfort when the cardinals come to visit, and they have been visiting a lot."

Paul Klitsch of Ashland, Pennsylvania shared:

"Whenever I see cardinals, I think of my dad. The cardinal that visits my house has been here for over 3 years. He taps at the front window, sits on the bush in front of it, and looks in the house. I named him Gerald, after my late father."

Laura Adams Rowland of Gretna, Virginia shared:

"Her last days, I asked her to come back and visit me as a butterfly or a bird so I would know she was ok. On bad days of missing her, I have had a cardinal come and sit on my shepherd's hook and just look inside. One also was at my 3 grandsons' bday cookout and stayed around them while they played. I truly believe it was my mama keeping her promise to me. After her death, every item that was given to me had cardinals on them. How ironic is that? I have always loved cardinals but now, even so much more."

Lola B of Chesterfield, Michigan shared:

"My mother would come and watch over me for months after she passed away. I would see her ever so often and in times of need. The past year was a rough time. I hadn't seen the cardinal. I recently had some scary health issues and I had a procedure done. Because of COVID, I had to go into the building alone. I was the first patient appointment for the day, so the parking lot was empty. There was the cardinal singing and coming closer. I was not alone after all. She came.

" My eyes welled up with tears and suddenly I knew I wasn't alone."

Dawn Zimmer Kennedy shared:

"I saw some cardinals after my mom's passing. There were just so many, it couldn't be a coincidence. It was the way they appeared that took my breath away that time. Sitting on top of a stop sign as I approached, one was literally flying along the side of my car on a rural road as I was driving. I was not having a good day and had to look twice. Another time I was walking and asked my mom 'If you're okay, please give me a sign.' I had actually forgotten it was almost at the end of my walk. There was the cardinal across on the sidewalk. I literally stopped and said 'mom if that's you, please come to me. Show me something.' The cardinal hopped towards the curb and flew right at me and around to a brush next to me. I actually have pictures in flight. I also have a cardinal tattooed on my wrist with the words handwritten from my mom on a card I once received that says "Believe it". These are just some appearances. I can honestly say they definitely comfort me sometimes inside but even then, it's just not enough."

Donna Kellett Bailey shared:

"*I lost my mom two years ago. It was the worst thing I could ever imagine, I then lost my husband the next year. Boy, did my world fall apart. We had been married 37 years together. I had heard the stories of cardinals which I believed with my whole heart. I have been visiting there many times. In fact, I had two at one time at my son's house. I have been having a really tough time, so they knew I needed to see them. Last night visiting with my dad, we were talking about my mom and Jerry and up above us, showed up a red cardinal. That's no coincidence.*"

"*I know every time I see a red cardinal, my youngest daughter has come to tell me she's okay now and that she has come to let me know*

we'll be together again one day. I'm also reminded of my dear sweet mother and my dearly departed husband. It's hard to tell which one is visiting me sometimes. I surely love it when I see red cardinals at my bird feeder and in my yard."

Carolyn Folk shared:

"*When I lost my Mama last year, a beautiful solid red bird came on the porch and looked at me. This beautiful bird didn't have a black mark on her. Then walked down the stairs and across the yard. My mama told me she will let me know she made it. My mama couldn't walk when she passed, so I believe it was her way of letting me know she is walking now.*"

Elva Enriquez shared:

"I lost my son three years ago. I was in so much grief about losing him, I moved to a new house and I saw some cardinals. Sometimes, I would see them near me. It was my son telling me he was ok now."

"I still have days I can hardly deal with but then I'll see that beautiful red bird and know he's got his eye on me."

Deborah Sanders Barksdale shared:

"My parents and my three brothers had all passed away. So when I saw cardinals, I would ask him which of my family were visiting. My husband passed away in July 2021 which was also our 41st wedding anniversary. I was so unbearably sad. A week later, it was his memorial and I could hardly bring myself to get ready to go. Finally, I was dressed and left but only got as far as our barn. There is a huge evergreen that we nurtured from a sprout when we first bought our property. I stopped at the tree and broke down and told my husband, Rush, that I just couldn't go. I missed him and couldn't bear going, so I turned around and went back to the house. All of a sudden, a cardinal swooped down, almost stopped dead in front of my windshield, and then landed in our tree on a lower branch watching me. I knew then it was him telling me I could do it and he was with me! He's always been my rock and I know he still is. I still have days I can hardly deal with but then, I'll see that beautiful red bird and know he's got his eye on me."

Marlene Walla shared:

"When my husband passed away in October 2018, it took four days for the rain to stop. Then I saw a beautiful male cardinal. My

sister-in-law on her birthday saw four cardinals, mom, dad, middle brother, and oldest brother. I cried when she told me."

Laura Rushing shared:

"My awesome husband and dad are with me. Every evening I sit outside, weather providing it's not raining or whatever, a male cardinal comes to my tree in the front yard and sings his head off. I love, love, love that baby."

Sally O'Brien Dillon of Cypress, Texas shared:

"Nearly two years ago, I was sitting on my patio in such terrible pain a day or so, after my husband of 58 years had died. I heard a noise on the roof behind me and then on the patio umbrella when suddenly, this beautiful cardinal peeked over the edge of the umbrella and stared right at me before flying away. I thought it was really strange as I had lived in this house for 15 years and sat on that patio every morning and evening and nothing like that had ever happened. The next day, I was in the same spot and suddenly, there came another beautiful cardinal and perched himself right on the top of the chair in front of me and looked right at me for several seconds before flying off. Later that day, I was back in the same place and just then, another beautiful cardinal flew onto the patio and perched right on top of the grill just beside me, once again, staring right at me before flying away. By then, I knew something was happening and immediately began to research cardinals and death. Well, of course, I found it immediately and I broke down and cried uncontrollably. The day after that, a group of 5 or 6 female cardinals gathered around my little waterfall pond that my husband really loved and they stayed for a while. Of course, I knew what had been taking place by then and the interesting thing is, since that day, I have only seen cardinals from a distance. I have never seen any cardinals before. None of them have even come close to the patio again as much as I would like them to. I guess their message had gotten through to me and now, they were staying at a distance. I thank God for sending them. It calmed my heart during some extremely difficult days. That experience was one I will never forget and now at those times when

I am overcome with grief, I try to remember those days and what they meant. True love really, really never dies."

Carol Circo Mackie shared:

"My Father in law passed away in 2000 of a bad heart. I was so fortunate to have such an unselfish and kind, loving, funny man for a father-in-law. He loved his family and his wife dearly and she was crazy about him. When my mother-in-law passed away 18 years later, I was sitting at my kitchen table with my oldest son. We looked out the window and saw a cardinal

"Cardinals are spirits bringing us messages from beyond."

pair. We hadn't seen them before and have not seen them since. I felt they were telling us they were together again and happy. Cardinals are spirits bringing us messages from beyond. I get chills every time I think of it."

Joyce Surchik of Romeo, Michigan shared:

"My husband died suddenly in December 2017. I believe in cardinals and the meaning that they bring angles and peace. I originally lived in Southwest Florida. I've never seen a cardinal in four and a half years. I moved to Michigan to be closer to family and still, haven't seen one. Yesterday, I walked past the door wall and I saw my first cardinal in a tree! I immediately said, is that you Steve? (My husband). I was so excited!"

Patricia Lutz Jones shared:

"I love cardinals. The first Christmas after my husband died, we were having Christmas with our daughter and we looked out on her porch railing was a beautiful cardinal, we all said it was dad

and was so sweet. Love those birds."

Ron and Ruth Macdougall of Meaford, Ontario shared:

"Thank you for sharing this. Cardinals were my late wife's favorite bird. Before she passed away in July of last year, we were living in a one-bedroom cottage that was beside a brook. The cardinals were nesting nearby, and they would sing a beautiful song. We had to move to another town and the first week of July, my wife of 48 years, 3 months, and 4 days passed away in my arms. I never heard another cardinal singing in a tree by my apartment. This was hard for me as April 15 would have been our 49th anniversary. The cardinal was my answer to the prayer that my wife was still alive in my heart, and would never leave me alone. I miss my wife very much, and although I haven't put anything in here, I just want to let everyone know that I love you all very much, and for giving me the strength to go on with my life. Thank you very much."

Billy Easley shared

"I lost my dearest best friend on Easter of last year. I cried every day for about 5 to 7 months and finally broke down and went to my doctor to get help. The pill just numbs me and my feelings. I feel like I didn't grieve appropriately. I have the cremated ashes and everything was willed to me. I still talk to him daily. I see cardinals on my mail routes daily but not sure if they are him. I keep asking for a sign to see if he's ok. Since his death, I have started collecting cardinals. Yes, the pain is still fresh. I'm still seeking peace and healing. I hope to find a support group or a real friend that I can talk to. It's difficult to take care of two fur babies and have to work all the time."

Kim Hughs Carter shared:

"My 25-year-old son, AJ, passed away tragically in November 2021. We both believed seeing cardinals were loved ones in heaven. I've prayed and prayed since his passing to see a cardinal. Yesterday, I received a call saying the police had arrested the man responsible for my son's death. Immediately, a red cardinal appears. I have no words. My son is at peace. Praise God From Whom All Blessings Flow."

LaRue McDonald Kyle shared the following stories:

"The 'Red Feathered Soul' is such a beautiful poem, thank you for sharing. My Mom passed away 35 years ago, and my sister 2 years ago who was my rock after mom died. Then last year, my only brother died. I love coming out on my deck and waiting for my cardinals to show up. I knew the saying that says "When Cardinals appear, Angels are near". My husband didn't know about it but one day while he was shopping for flowers for our yard, he came across the most beautiful wind chimes with that saying and cardinals on each chime and surprised me on my birthday with it. It was then that I told him I see cardinals all the time and now, he talks to them too."

"I love cardinals. I lost a husband and son within a three year span. I have bird feeders up and cardinals come at the right time every time. It brings so much peace to my soul. I collected a few cardinal things and they bring me back to God and the love I miss, especially my son. I know he is near. Every one of my friends knows of my love for these amazing birds that God created. I have many pictures of cardinals on my phone and look at them often. They don't stay

around long but long enough for me to get a picture which I praise God for. I love your site and am so glad I found it. I also have an autoimmune disease and issues with depression, anxiety, and panic attacks. These visits from cardinals sure do help. Praying you feel better and that God brings you peace through your many losses. God bless you."

Gloria Shelato-Miller of Somersworth, New Hampshire shared:

"I see cardinals all the time. I lost my husband, Roger, 8 years ago, my daughter, Lisa, 4 years ago, and my Mom, Ila, 3 years ago. I love and miss them every day but I will see them again."

Eileen Young of Erie, Pennsylvania shared:

"My husband of 47 years passed away in January 2021. He died from COVID-19. Later than a year in March, my daughter came from Alabama to stay with me for a while. We were sitting in the living room and a beautiful red cardinal attached himself to the screen and stayed there for a while. I have lived in this spot for 45 years. It has never happened before. Also later that day, we were walking in a wooded park and the cardinal followed us everywhere. I made a little tribute to my hubby, as he was a Vietnam War veteran, in the living room. I have his urn, a picture, a Vietnam ball cap, and the whole time I was putting this together, a red cardinal was sitting on the fence singing the whole time, it was so amazing."

Kathy Inpa Fuller shared:

"The other day was the 7th anniversary of my mom going home, and I was really missing her. A couple of years later, my sister went home. So it was a sad day for me. I was looking out the back door and there was a beautiful red male and beautiful female cardinal

family playing in my lilac tree! They were telling me that mom and Bonnie were okay and to not be sad. The 'Red Feathered Soul' by Elle Bee is such a lovely poem."

Whitney Cattle shared:

"I started having a cardinal show up at my house right after my best friend passed away from cancer in September of 2020. Anytime I'd struggle and wish that my best friend was still here to talk to, the cardinal would fly by my dining room window and then sit on the branches of the closest little tree."

Teresa Mitusina shared:

"In November of 2005, my husband passed, while I was in my room crying uncontrollably for a very long time, a cardinal appeared on a tree branch directly by my window facing me, it distracted me from all the crying because the bird stayed for a very long time and that's kinda unusual, I felt that it was my husband's spirit came to comfort me."

Denise Nugent shared:

"In December 2017, my brother passed away from liver cancer. He was only 56 years old. It was so devastating to our whole family. A couple of days after he passed away, a cardinal showed up on my front porch. This cardinal sat in one spot and stared at me through our glass door for about 10 minutes and then flew away. I was so overwhelmed that I started recording it on my phone. I really believe that it was my brother letting me know that he was okay. This gave me comfort and peace."

Marilou Craft shared:

"Such a beautiful poem. I lost my brother in September to lung cancer. I also lost both my parents over 20 years ago. My brother's

passing has shown me how short life is as I miss him so much. I have asked him for signs letting me know he's okay. Well, he answered me a few weeks ago, when a cardinal appeared outside my bedroom window. He's there most of the day flying into the window with his beak, if I'm in the kitchen I hear him outside my brother's window. It's weird but now I'm afraid of the cardinal leaving. I mean it's there from sun up to sun down. I thought losing my parents was hard but this is such a different loss. I was born into a large family of seven brothers and a sister. I'm so afraid of losing another sibling which I know is bound to happen. Thank you for sharing your story. I now know they always remain with us."

Carolyn Herr shared*:*

"October 1st was our 55th wedding anniversary. A cardinal appeared in the tree by my patio. I never saw a cardinal in that tree before or since."

Judy Hillhouse shared:

"My sister and I were my mom's caregivers. The day she passed, she was home. I lived across the street from her and I was called over there because she named me her medical decision-maker. I gave her morphine and was advised within seconds that she was gone. I went outside to call the rest of the family and to get my emotions in order when all of a sudden, a hawk landed on her ramp right in front of me. The spirituality of a hawk is to protect and give you strength. Now, mind you there were not any hawks in the area around her house. Until that day, it hasn't been around. But a red cardinal and his mate are always in my trees. The day my mom passed, I needed strength and protection. I very much believe in the spiritual meaning behind birds. My house is full of cardinal's knick knacks. The more I can get, the closer I feel to my mom."

Patsy Rheam shared:

"I lost my 34-year-old daughter in 1970. Shortly after she died, I noticed a beautiful cardinal would appear on our deck a lot. Then one day, I saw it on the back of a deck chair looking through a window. I truly believe that is Kim's spirit watching me; trying to let me know she is waiting for me."

Eleanor Martin shared:

"My husband was very sick. One day, he told me he needed to be free. So this red cardinal came to tell me that now, he is. Thank you. Now spread your wings and fly."

Maureen O'Malley-MacKinnon shared:

"I saw a cardinal visit recently when I was feeling down and missing my parents, especially with the recent loss of our beautiful dog, Monti."

Virginia Presnell shared:

"I lost my husband to the virus in April 2021. We were married 49 years and I miss him. I didn't get to see him in the hospital for 5 weeks. I feel so bad that I couldn't be with him. We lost our only child, our daughter, to a car accident in July 2015. He was my rock through all these years. We are raising our grandchildren due to the fact that she didn't marry a good man like her father. I did see a beautiful cardinal the other day from my kitchen window sitting on the wire, just looking around at the yard and even in the window. I got so happy thinking it was my husband or daughter. I lost my mom the same year as my daughter in March 2015, and then, my brother two years later to Parkinson's. I lost my dad 10 years ago and my baby brother 8 years ago—my whole family. So when I see a cardinal, I wish it to be any of my loved ones. But I miss my soulmate, my husband. He was so wonderful."

Cynthia Pearce shared:

"We have had two cardinals visiting us daily since our son, Craig, passed away. Our sign from heaven that he is still around!"

Kathy Freeman of Belton, South Carolina shared:

"My Daughter was killed 3 weeks ago today and I have had about ten cardinals showing up in my yard ever since she died. They are our angels."

"I won't be far my soul live on, With every sunset and every dawn."

Dean Bumgardner of Thomasville, North Carolina shared:

"I saw a cardinal in my front yard this morning and my sister, Becky, passed away last night. I guess that was her looking out for me."

Jeanie Shell of Evansville, Indiana shared:

"Since Dince, my husband died, I've seen 20 of them red cardinals. He is telling me 'Babe, I'm ok. Please be happy, and don't cry anymore."

Connie Peterson Safly shared,

I also had a really neat experience with a cardinal. My husband of 42 years suddenly left me with no warning. I came home from work to find a note and he and all of his belongings were gone. The next morning, divorce papers were delivered by the sheriff's office. I was so devastated. As I lay in bed crying my eyes out the next morning, I kept hearing a noise at the window. I finally got up and looked out the window to see a beautiful red cardinal on the window ledge. He kept cocking his head at me and staring at me. We sat there for a long time just looking at each other until I finally calmed down and decided to get up and fix myself a cup of tea. As I went to the kitchen on the other side of the house, I looked up and there was the cardinal in the window. Just to let you know I had never had a cardinal in my yard before this time. He sat there watching me while I fixed my tea; then followed me to the dining room window where I sat and drank my tea. As we watched each other, I had the strangest feeling that my mother was there comforting me and letting me know I was not alone. It was so comforting. This beautiful bird continued to follow me from window to window the entire morning. The cardinal finally flew away towards the evening when my children and others started arriving but I have never forgotten the comfort it gave me. I now have a huge cardinal collection in my home that I truly treasure and it always reminds me of the day. It assured me that my mother will always be watching over me

80

Chapter Three
"Angels in Flight"

After the gift of the Red Feathered Soul experience and the launch of that poem, is when more magic really started happening. Customers would reach out to me and share their stories of visits from their loved ones. The first one after the Red Feathered Soul was a request for a bluejay theme poem as this woman who lost her son in a car accident, said he came as a bluejay after he passed away. She said her son shared the personality of the bluejay and the timing of the visits confirmed it was him. This is how "The Blue Feathered Soul" was born. The next poem came from a lady who lost her beloved sister and best friend who faithfully visits as a monarch butterfly, thus giving birth to the "Butterfly Spirit" version. I hope you enjoy these stories and some of the poem card designs. They are truly beautiful and give us so much hope. It has been such an amazing gift that these people have given us with their stories and opening up their hearts.

Blue Feathered Soul

I'll come one day to visit you,
You'll know it's me and feel it too.
I'll be blue, joyful, free,
And sing my startling melody.
There's no mistake I'll come that day,
I feel your pain, you've lost your way.
I love you so and miss you too,
Our hearts entwined, our bond is true.
Just close your eyes, you'll see my face,
No time nor space can take your place.
But it's still your turn so take every chance,
To live with wonder, to sing, and dance.
Know every problem in life will pass,
This journey's short, so live, love, laugh.
Please don't despair, we're not apart,
I'll always live inside your heart.
Life moves fast, one day you'll see,
We'll meet again, it's destiny.

- Elle Bee

Eric Kennedy shared:

"I had an experience with these majestic birds. A very close friend passed at 5:00 PM and at that very moment, a blue jay came out of nowhere. Very bizarre. Before she passed, she said she'd send me a bluebird. This is a true story!"

"I'll be blue, joyful, free, And sing my startling melody."

Barbara Foor of Pataskala, Ohio shared:

"I have received several visits from a cardinal and I did receive a blue jay feather outside of the driver's side door of Tristan's Blue Dodge truck."

Susan of Grosse Pointe, Michigan shared:

"My best friend lost her son. He was just out of high school and died in a car crash. His personality was larger than life and he would light up a room when he walked in. Since his death, a blue jay comes sweeping into her yard saying 'cawwww, cawwwww'. She knows it is him, and it brings tears to her eyes."

Peggy Hart shared:

"I finally saw my first cardinal this morning since my sister died in November. I was so excited, I cried. It flew right in front of me. And the most beautiful blue jay was right behind it. My sister's death has been so hard. She was my very best friend."

Kerry Barrett of Parsons, Tennessee shared:

"My daddy had COPD. Sometimes, he would get outside for the early feeding of the birds. His neighbor will help him instead of

him doing the steps by himself. It can get difficult. So daddy sat a jar of seed on the table on the porch every morning. Thomas would bring his paper to the table and pour the seed on an old ironing board my daddy fed them on. I loved seeing him do it everyday. He had a blue jay and cardinal that came every day (and also a squirrel). When he passed away in 2010, I went back to his grave a few hours after the funeral. There were no trees right around his grave. There was a line of trees about a hundred yards or more. But I had been there several times visiting my stepmother and we had the funeral under three oak trees elsewhere in the cemetery and I had never seen a bird nearby. That day, as I had been there for about two minutes, a cardinal didn't just fly by, the cardinal circled my daddy's grave. I have never witnessed anything like that before. I just cried and said 'There's your cardinal daddy.'"

Suzy Lang-vuletich shared:

"My dad passed away in 1995. I used to see blue jays since then. For the first time in a long time, I saw that there's one big large blue jay in our tree today. I feel my dad was telling me all is ok and he is looking out for my son, his grandson, my Nicky. It's a good day today."

Jenni C. of Louisiana shared:

"My dad died unexpectedly and I found out on Friday afternoon. Friday morning before work, I saw the biggest blue jay hopping around by my door. I smiled and talked to him and he flew into the trees. I know it was my dad, and I usually don't believe in that stuff. The bird was 100% him. When I was little, we would watch blue jays together in our backyard, and to encourage me to eat, he would take my spoon and say "show me how a little baby blue bird eats!" It's definitely not a coincidence! There were no flowers or seeds or any reason why a big blue jay would want to come right up to my door like that and wait for me." together.

Priscilla Staton of Stuarts Draft, Virginia shared:

"My mother passed away in April 2022. I have seen my cardinals. One day, I was outside at home and a cardinal and blue jay were playing. Mind you, my mother loved both of those birds."

"It was as if he was comforting us the last two days before he passed away."

This was a letter sent to me through social media from a customer. I asked if I could share their story. They shared images of a blue jay landing on each of them. I was awestruck.

Renee W. of Tennessee shared:

"I have been trying to find a downloadable version of the 'Blue Feathered Soul' poem card by Elle Bee. I wanted to use it in a celebration of life for my brother that passed. I love the entire thing with the bird. This holds a special meaning for me and my siblings. While my brother was in the bed dying, we had a blue jay come visit us. We were all in awe as he climbed on each of us; my sister-in-law, my niece, my other brother, and my sister. We have never experienced anything like it. It was as if he was comforting us the last two days before he passed away."

The Butterfly Spirit

Butterfly Spirit

I've come to seek you out today,
I feel your pain, you've lost your way.
I've never left I live through you.
Our hearts entwined, our bond is true.
No time nor space can take away,
The love we share will always stay.
Thank you for still loving me,
I am everywhere and finally free.
It's still your turn so take every chance,
To live with wonder, to sing and dance.
I won't be far my soul lives on,
With every sunset and every dawn.
I'll be your sign, just look for me.
I am still with you eternally.

- Elle Bee

Kenneth Reese of Austin, Texas shared:

> *"Before my wife passed three years ago, she loved her butterflies and cardinals. Rest In Heaven."*

Elizabeth Babineaux of Church Point, Louisiana shared:

> *"I have had butterflies all around me today. I know my daddy is happy being with my momma and brother now."*

Jeanne Elliott of Vero Beach, Florida shared:

> *"My brave and beautiful daughter, Lynn, is a delicate yellow butterfly that will flit around me in places known to us both. Forever 17, Silver Girl!"*

Carol Hanan Meyeroff shared:

> *"That is beautiful. Cardinals are definitely a sign from a loved one in heaven. As I always say, 'ya gotta believe'. I lost my daughter five years ago and the cardinals and butterflies bring me comfort."*

Linda Youngquist shared:

> *"I lost my husband in April 2021. I was sitting on my front porch talking to my husband. I told him I could not do this alone. I told him he had to show me a sign that he was with me. It wasn't very long before white butterflies started coming. They were all over. I know this is him watching over me."*

Laura Tice Thielke of Wausau Wisconsin shared:

"The first birthday I had, after my mother passed away 11 years ago was rough. It was October, my 57th birthday. I'd been feeling down all day. I was leaving work and walking to my car. It was a bit dreary but breezy. I saw what I thought were old leaves fluttering in the breeze, then I realized at least, one was a butterfly! In October, in the Midwest–unheard of. I took it as a message from my mother to not feel forgotten, that she is still here with us, especially on my birthday. Can I swear that there was a butterfly? No, but I did look again and again and am convinced it was there. Either way, the message was received and I felt warm and loved for the rest of the day and I always associate butterflies with my mother. I have a beautiful wind chime that hangs on her back porch in my bathroom, so in warmer weather, I can open the window and hear the beautiful sound, and the rest of the decor features butterflies and flowers."

Mary Ann Denny of Leander, Texas shared:

"My mother always was feeding her cardinals. Even when she moved over 200 miles, she had cardinals in the backyard. She got sick and in the hospital with a brain bleed and got confused easily. As we sat there talking, she started staring out the window. I asked her what she was looking at out the window. She said the birds. I asked what kind of birds. Her answer was the cardinals, of course. I should have taken that as a sign that she did not have long to be here as she was being visited by loved ones ready for her to come home. For Christmas that year, my caregiver bought me rugs for my apartment and put them down while I was gone. When I returned home, I was greeted by the bright red

cardinals on the rug. I knew immediately that my mother was there for me as she had always been. I don't look for signs from people that have passed, but I definitely do receive them from time to time. Cardinals, butterflies, and neon orange fingernail polish."

Mary Baker shared:

"So sorry about everyone's loss. My mother, Patti, and I just love butterflies. I will always say 'Look! Your mom stopped by to say hello.' She is always with us."

Barbara Gupton of Omaha, Nebraska shared:

"I usually feel cardinals are my angels. However, I have one special friend who passed, and from the first day, I began seeing butterflies. I always associate those with this special friend."

Janet Billington of Atchison, Kansas shared:

"I have both cardinals and butterflies around me all the time. After my friend passed, I went outside to just sit and tell her that I appreciated her friendship. Suddenly, a butterfly landed on my hand and nibbled on it for a long time. I just smiled knowing it was her."

Marquritta Pearl Uelese shared:

"Four days after we buried my dad, we visited his grave around seven in the evening. We played music and sang there. And then, a beautiful white butterfly flew from under the cross on top of his grave."

Jeannie Soldavini Johnson of Oceano, California shared:

"My son visited me the other day when two male monarchs landed on me."

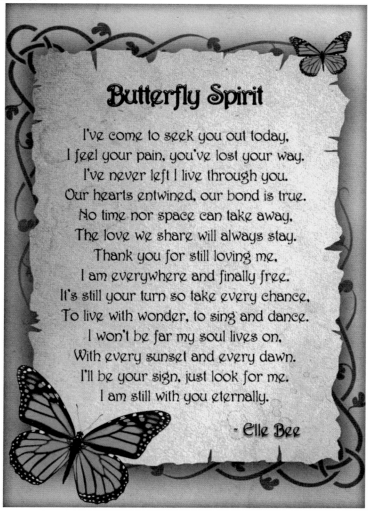

Butterfly Spirit

I've come to seek you out today,
I feel your pain, you've lost your way.
I've never left I live through you.
Our hearts entwined, our bond is true.
No time nor space can take away,
The love we share will always stay.
Thank you for still loving me,
I am everywhere and finally free.
It's still your turn so take every chance,
To live with wonder, to sing and dance.
I won't be far my soul lives on,
With every sunset and every dawn.
I'll be your sign, just look for me.
I am still with you eternally.

- Elle Bee

Barb W. of Saint Clair Shores, Michigan shared:

"I lost my dear friend and confidant, my sister, two years ago to cancer. Ever since then, whenever I return to my cottage up north, she appears as a monarch butterfly and sits on the bow of my rowboat. She never misses. I just know it is her."

"I've never left, I live through you, Our hearts entwined, our bond is true."

Darlene Groff shared:

"My angels in flight sign are butterflies. At my husband's graveside service, a butterfly landed on the pastor's Bible and stayed the whole service."

Jennifer Richardson-Greaud of Greenwood, Louisiana shared:

"Butterfly Spirit is a perfect poem for our aching hearts. My daughter-in-law passed away in 2012. She was just 40. Cancer knows no age. She was my best friend and really like a daughter. We would watch butterflies as we sat outside with our glass of wine. Everywhere I moved, no matter how far, the most beautiful black with striking blue butterfly has been following me. I know this is Claire."

Nicolette B. of Georgia shared:

So the story goes, after my sister died of breast cancer, there is a blue butterfly that continues to visit me and my mom quite frequently. It once stayed with her for nearly two hours once while she was mowing the lawn and it brings us comfort to know she is here with us always.

Patti Looney of Simsbury, Connecticut shared:

"Not a cardinal story but this butterfly was hanging around my mom's Chrysanthemums we planted together years ago. It still blooms and the butterflies come back every year even after transplanting the flowers to my yard. My mom passed away around Christmas and each year, I feel so sad, especially around this time of year. Seeing this butterfly made my day. It's the smallest of signs that make the biggest impact."

KD De Leon of Rizal Province in the Philippines shared:

"I lost a very close friend, a confidant, in 2016 from HIV complications. He died at a very young age of 25. His death due to the virus has opened so much needed conversation among us friends about knowing one's status. He is the reason why whenever I buy an iPhone, I choose the red variant. The red purchases contribute to the Global Fund's support of AIDS programs and I do it as a tribute to him. Despite being a little afraid of flying insects, I will sometimes feel calm and a smile will just come whenever I see a fluttering butterfly. Especially, if it's a white one, I know it's my friend trying to say hi and reminding me he never forgets and is still here with me in spirit. I often see signs of him when I am very happy. As we are both very happy people and have shared so many fun moments just laughing at our inside jokes, looking like fools to everyone. I just miss him so much and his impact on us, his friends, is more valuable than he could ever know. He saved us."

Kiel Agut of Taguig City in the Philippines shared:

"We lost our beloved daddy in 2010. Growing up as the eldest, only son, the only brother to 2 sisters, and being gay, I have felt that my dad has not always accepted me for who I am. I feel that I was just being tolerated. Up until his sudden death, we have not talked about my true self. But on the day of his funeral, a white butterfly landed on my shoulder. Like a dad putting his arms over his son's shoulder trying to say everything is okay but cannot enunciate the words exactly. Tears just fell from my eyes. I know it's dad saying I may not have openly come out to him, but he accepts me as me and nothing will ever change that he is my dad and I am his only son."

"I know it's my friend trying to say hi and reminding me he never forgets and is still here with me in spirit."

Leanne Labonte of Calumet, Michigan shared:

"We had a butterfly fly around us all 2 years ago in a funeral. The butterfly buzzed down each row and twice around my only grandbaby. It was my and my mom's farewell meeting."

"*I am still with you eternally.*"

Lovie Cabangon of Rizal Province in the Philippines shared:

"My father and I have always had a special relationship because I am the youngest daughter of four siblings. I can say that I am a daddy's girl. So I was really devastated when my father died of several health complications due to old age. But my dad will not be there whenever it's my mother's birthday. We will always see butterflies or moths fluttering around our celebration. It has happened so often that we will sometimes joke around it, telling on it when it comes around a little later than usual. But nevertheless, we have always associated butterflies with my father visiting and it always brings joy to us."

JK Favila shared:

"Our first born daughter was born with congenital heart disease. We were told later in the pregnancy of my wife that the likeliness of her survival is very low. She was almost a stillbirth but she fought, and together we fought with her in her battle. But her helpless little body is only able to handle so much, the Lord took her only three weeks after she was born. It was not her time to be with us. And although we were able to properly set our expectations, it still pains me and my wife that we were not able to let her feel our love for her for a long time. A month after our baby's funeral, we visited her grave only to see that a flower had bloomed beside her grave and a white butterfly was flying around it. When we came closer and closer to our baby's gravestone, the butterfly settled in the stone, and stayed there for a few seconds while opening and closing its wings. My wife said to me it's our daughter, waiting for us. She knows we will visit her as often as we can and she was there to welcome us."

"Thank you for still loving me, I am everywhere and finally free."

The Hummingbird Spirit

Hummingbird Spirit

I've come to seek you out today,
I feel your pain, you've lost your way.
I've never left I live through you.
Our hearts entwined, our bond is true.
No time nor space can take away,
The love we share will always stay.
Thank you for still loving me,
I am everywhere and finally free.
It's still your turn so take every chance,
To live with wonder, to sing and dance.
I won't be far my soul lives on,
With every sunset and every dawn.
I'll be your sign, just look for me.
I am still with you eternally.

- Elle Bee

Jenny-Mike Laney shared:

"I know where everyone's coming from. When my daddy passed four years ago, everything was all about cardinals and hummingbirds and their signs of hope that my dad is okay."

"Everything was all about cardinals and hummingbirds and their signs of hope that my dad is okay."

Barbara Zielsdorf shared:

"Hummingbirds are signs, too. I say hi to my mom in heaven every time I see one.

Ronda Dana Wolfley shared:

"Unfortunately, there are no cardinals in our area. But after my father passed, a hummingbird came and literally kissed my daughter and flew around her head. My father loved watching hummingbirds. I believe all birds are little messengers."

Heather Suggs of Arizona shared:

"What is amazing about grief is that despite the difficulties in the relationship, no matter how hard the struggles were, you still grieve. There is a feeling that the person you lost is no longer suffering and is back to a place of peace, back to the very best version of themselves. Somehow that translates into my heart as peace as well. My mother had a hard life and struggled. I know she did her best. I miss and love her so much. I have seen hummingbirds since she passed. The timing is always more than coincidental."

Author: When I was speaking with Heather about her story, a hummingbird appeared!! It was incredible.

Carin Tompkins of Erie, Illinois shared:

"I had a similar experience as everyone after my father died. It was a hummingbird that greeted me at my living room window for three days in a row. It let me know that my father was still watching over me."

"It's still your turn so take every chance, To live with wonder, to sing and dance."

Chapter Three
"Other Angel Signs"

The Angel's Sign

I'll come one day to visit you,
You'll know it's me and feel it too.
An angel sign is what you'll see,
It represents my soul is free.
There is no mistake I'll come that day.
I feel your pain, you've lost your way.
Cardinals and Blue Jays, other angels in flight,
Pennies or feathers will appear in plain sight.
Butterflies, dragonflies, songs from our past,
Will appear through your life
'til we're together at last.
I love you so and miss you too,
And only want the best for you.
It's still your turn so take every chance,
To live with wonder, to sing and dance.
I am not far my soul lives on,
With every sunset and every dawn.
I'll be your sign, just look for me.
My spirit is with you eternally.

-Elle Bee

There is this amazingly haunting and beautiful Chinese idiom that reads "One Day, Three Autumns". As I read it, I was overcome with emotion. Yes, I thought, one day missing someone feels like 3 years. That time can stand still in those moments of grief like time has never stood still before. Please, know these moments will pass, I promise you, they will pass. There is no denying our connection to those we love never dies. Still, there is more than just the connection that exists in our hearts. In the stories I have had the honor of hearing, as well as my own experiences, there are angel signs everywhere. The signs are usually involved with special timing or hearing a song that was a memory connected with that person, pennies, feathers, or just signs from the person will appear. I know someone who smells her mother's perfume. It doesn't happen often but when it does, there is no denying it was her. It was usually at times of despair or feeling lost.

My grandmother, who I never met, died of cancer at the age of 36. My mother was only 14 when her mother passed away. Years later, as my mother was laying on her bed crying herself to sleep, she felt her bed shift and a hand on her shoulder. It was brief but the feeling was unmistakable. She knew it was her mother. I should note that my mother was not super-spiritual in that sense. She was not someone who was "in tune" with the spiritual side of things outside of going to a Catholic school before she had to quit, to help raise her siblings. She had one more experience with her mother. She was home alone, and she woke up in the middle of the night from noise. As she listened, she heard it again, it was the sound of high heel shoes walking on the upstairs floor. My Grandma was not tall and wore them all the time. My mother got up to see if her sister came home, or if perhaps, her aunt was over. It was neither. Mom never had any more stories to share, perhaps because she didn't know how to look for other signs because I am sure her mother never left her side or her father who died a few years later. One time when I was in my early 20s, we went to Canada to visit my grandmother's grave site. We had trouble finding the cemetery because it was now 4 times the size and across the street from one another. My mother hadn't been there since she was very young. We just decided to wander in. Suddenly, I felt called to a certain area. I walked straight to it without even looking at the other tombstones. My mother always referred to her as Vera. I had no idea her name was Mary Vera. I found her stone. There is no doubt that she led us to her site. The look on my mother's face when she was reunited with her mother's site, was so beautiful. I remember feeling the spirit surrounding us.

I had a very special angel visit, that was from my brother who passed away. It was our song. I was listening to music, which was a completely different genre of music and suddenly, YouTube started playing this song. I stopped what I was doing. I looked out the window and there was the cardinal, his birthday was the next day. I have a dear friend whose son's sports number "33", shows up at the most needed times. There are no rules, you will see signs of things that represent them, their personality, your shared memories, and love.

Last but certainly not least, angel signs will also show up in people. You will be sent angels here. Just as I was chosen as the vehicle for the poems, people everywhere including you will be called to be someone's angel and source of comfort. Never underestimate the miracle of sharing your pain and your story of how you made it through, passing on hope, or helping someone who is lost. We are all here to help each other heal. Listen to your callings.

This next chapter is filled with other stories of angel sign visits. I hope that this will help you all know how to start looking. There are no coincidences, only synchronicities. Spirit is everywhere.

Theresa Trail shared:

"When my dad passed, all the family had ladybugs come to us. One of my nieces had them all over her bed when she got home. I had them on my porch, too. Just before he died, my mom sent me home to get something and a bird landed on top of my car as I was starting to get in and just stared at me. Well, he passed right about that time my mom told me. I think it was my dad trying to let me know it was okay."

Eunice Guy Walker shared:

"My oldest of three sons had a horrible auto accident at age 18. His human body couldn't sustain the injuries, and four days later, he was gone. After many agonizing months, I heard the doves cooing while sitting outside. It honestly seemed like Gary saying,

"An angel sign is what you'll see, It represents my soul is free."

"Mom, I'm okay". I felt such a warm feeling as if a blanket was wrapped around me. It was then that I began to recover from this hateful disease called grief. Recovery is a constant, and I am a recovering bereaved parent by choice."

Carol Hanan Meyeroff shared:

"So sorry for everyone's loss. Look for cardinals, pennies, beautiful clouds, and sunsets, all signs. My daughter sent me a sign right after she died. About a hundred blackbirds flew into a tree in my neighbors backyard and were squawking very loudly. I was sitting in my backyard alone. A few minutes later, my friend came into my yard and asked what the noise was. I told her to look up at the tree. She was amazed also by the number of birds. We both said out loud, could that be a sign from my daughter? And at that moment, all the birds flew out of the tree and into the clouds and three birds circled my house and flew off to join the others. It left me and my friend speechless and we both cried knowing it was a sign from my daughter. Look for the signs and you will find them. I hope they will bring you peace and comfort as they do for me."

L. Bissonette shared:

I too have experienced angel signs that are so amazing they cannot be denied. It was my first birthday after my mother had passed away. She would always be the first person to wish me Happy Birthday. As I laid in bed, I heard something lightly fall over on my dresser. As I looked over, it was the last birthday card my mother had gotten me. She actually wrote in it which was very odd because she was having some dementia. What she wrote was very special to me because she told me to be good to myself and how much she loved me. I kept that card on my dresser along with the last Christmas card she wrote for me. I still can't believe it happened. It hasn't happened since but it was so amazing.

Aaron Washington of Gary, Indiana shared:

"My mom passed away in December 2021. Shortly after her burial, I was finding white feathers, 2021 dimes, and 2021 pennies everywhere. They seem to just appear in places I had just walked over. I'd turn around and there they are, a large white feather appeared in a sterile hospital environment. How could that just be a coincidence? I do not think so."

Deborah Williams Hamilton of Noble, Oklahoma shared:

"The winter after my mother passed, we had deep snow. We had a huge cedar tree in our front yard that was covered with snow. I looked out the window and it was covered with these red cardinals. They were all over the tree. Looked just like a beautiful Christmas card. This was in the winter of 1992, so we didn't have iPhones like we do today. Unfortunately, I didn't have a camera either. Wish I could have captured that moment. Momma's birthday is on the eleventh of September. I'm always finding eleven cents (a dime and a penny). I feel like those are hugs from my mom letting me know she's still near."

"The love we share will always stay"

Barbara Klein of Orange, Texas shared:

"My son in law found me a feather right outside my door as we were going to my husband's graveside."

Linda Biamonte of Port Alberni, British Columbia shared:

"Feathers seem to be my sign from heaven. I have found many feathers this past year since I lost my dad. I miss him a lot. "

Freida M. shared:

"I understand what everyone is talking about. My kids and I think whenever a dragonfly comes around, it is my daughter. My cousin is that way about eagles."

L. Belanger of St. Clair Shores, Michigan shared:

"My mother, who was my best friend, passed away the same year I turned 50. It was like there was this entire shift in my life. It is hard to even put it into words as I was also a caretaker for her. One day, I was feeling so sad and heavy. I should add that all of her siblings had also passed, my father too. That day, I went outside to get some air. I couldn't prepare for what I saw. I saw this group of the largest birds I have ever seen in my entire life. They landed on my neighbor's roof directly across from me. They were looking at me. It was phenomenal. I waved at them and they swirled over my head. I just know it was them."

"Cardinals and Blue Jays, other angels in flight, Pennies or feathers will appear in plain sight."

Ann Marie of Michigan shared:

"I will never forget losing this lady at work who was like a second mother to me. She had and has a place in my heart that will always be hers. Noreen was so full of life and passion. I was heartbroken when she died suddenly. Months later, I was walking into work and this bird was trying to land on me. Nothing like that had ever happened before. I left for lunch and came back, the same bird came back and tried to communicate with me. Later that day, I looked on my calendar and it was Earth Day, her birthday. I was amazed. When I left to go home that day, the bird came back. I never saw that bird again. I know in my heart it was her. After all these years, I am still missing her, and am so amazed by that day."

Ken Ordonez of Rizal Province in the Philippines shared:

"Being the first grandchild in the family, my grandpa and I have an amazing relationship. We are both intellectuals and like learning new things. He was very excited to be able to attend my graduation being the first of his grandchildren to be able to graduate college but at the time, his health was already deteriorating and he always needed aid to even get up the bed. So I just brought the graduation to him and made sure he sees me in my graduation robe and cap. He stayed in our home for the last few months he lived. But when he died in 2015, I was at work on a night shift. My aunt called me and I bolted out of the office to go home and be with the family. I was hoping I could still get to tell him my parting words, but I was too late. My grandpa died peacefully in his sleep beside my grandma. Weeks after his funeral, we were cleaning the room where they stayed during his last few days and I saw the side of a thick book with a feather in it being used as a bookmark. I pulled it from the pile and it was the dictionary my grandpa gave me as a Christmas gift. He was always giving me gifts like puzzles, books, and other things I can use to learn. And at the time that he gave me that dictionary, mobile phones, and the Internet were already the go-to when trying to find the meaning of a word. But I have valued that book ever since. Now, whenever the family is together, especially when celebrating a special occasion, we will often see a brown butterfly, sort of a big moth, and it is always that kind of butterfly. We just knew it was him wanting to join us and letting us know he is still with us in spirit."

Jao Anthony of Gumaca, Province of Quezon in the Philippines:

"My mother raised me by herself, we were not that well off, and to top it off, I can be considered a miracle baby because she gave birth to me late in life. We were living in the suburbs but I had to go to the city to work after I graduated college. It was hard living alone and far away from my only rock, but I have to do it for us and our dreams. But January 2018, the day I am most afraid of, came. I immediately made arrangements for me to be able to go home to our province. Riding the bus home, I was just blank. Upon reaching our street, I saw our house, full of lights. There are a lot of people. And there was mom, lying peacefully in her beautiful white coffin. I don't know what to feel. I was too overwhelmed to even cry. I just have to process everything that the queen of my life is now in heaven. A few weeks later, I had to go back to the city. I had to get back to work while trying to get back to normal. As I was about to ride the bus, a white jasmine flower fell on top of my luggage. But what's weird is there weren't any jasmine plants nearby. Only some non-fruit bearing trees. The smell of the jasmine is so fresh, reminiscent of my mom's hugs when I was a kid. Right there, I knew my mom would always be guiding me and watching over me. I kept that jasmine flower, of course. I have a tattoo now in my arms that says "Long Live The Queen" and then my mom's name. And a jasmine flower, too."

Dan Christian of Pasig City in the Philippines shared:

"I remember when my boyfriend passed away in 2016 due to Pneumonia and Asthma complications, I will always see things that remind me of him, the second any memory of him crosses my mind. For example, I will just remember suddenly how we got matching koi fish tattoos or maybe I was just sharing that fact with a friend, and suddenly, I will see something that has koi in it. Like a keychain, or a painting. Well, koi fish really reminds me of him. But other things that let me know he is trying to say hi to me are a sudden cold breeze, butterflies, and Volkswagen Beetle cars."

"Butterflies, dragonflies, songs from our past, Will appear through your life until we're together at last."

Angel Curativo shared:

"We lost our dad from diabetes complications back in December of 2019. Prior to his demise, we were almost already living in the hospital. We were preparing ourselves for the worst but we are almost always on our knees in prayer for a miracle to happen. It was still very hard for us when my dad passed, especially for my mom who's now also very old. In the Philippines, we have a superstition that a person's spirit will stay on earth wandering for 40 days before it finally enters its final destination. And on the 40th day, loved ones will usually have a celebration, feast, or a simple tribute, coupled with prayers for finally, the spirit of the departed will now enter heaven. So as a typical Filipino family, we did our tribute. But little do we know, ours will be a little bit more special and memorable. That day, the weather was not very nice. It was raining the entire morning and cloudy in the afternoon. We

went to the cemetery around 3 pm and it was still a little gloomy at that time. But as soon as we get there, the clouds started to part and there came the sun. We did not take it as a big deal at first. We just thought we were lucky and that we can have our celebration in better weather at least. But then, my little brother suddenly screamed. He saw a rainbow. We finally took it as a sign that my dad is finally free and glad that we were there for him to send him on his final journey. Because of that day, we will always recall this story whenever we see a rainbow and I am glad we have something truly magical and celestial to remind us of our dad."

Justine De Leon of Antipolo City shared:

"We lost 3 fur baby dogs in one month due to a parvovirus outbreak. We have lost half of the 6 dogs we have and it was truly a devastating time for the entire family. It was also very sudden. The night we lost the 3rd dog was the worst time for me. I broke down as I cannot accept the reality and for me, it was so unfair. I felt guilty, too. I kept blaming myself for not being a  *better fur parent to them. One morning, I just woke up crying because the fur babies visited me in my dream. I was playing catch with them with the exact ball we use. I threw the ball one last time but they all came back to me with a rose in each of their mouths. I can remember it so clearly. They dropped the rose in my hand one by one, let out one bark, and ran away to the fields. I was just screaming their names in my dreams until I cried in my dreams and woke up with tears in my eyes. At first, I was sad. I wanted to go back to sleep so I could play with them again. But after a while, I realized it was their way of saying 'It's okay. We are happy where we are and we are happy with the short time you are our fur parents.' They were thanking me. They didn't want me to be*

burdened anymore. And much like how they console me when I was sad when they were still alive, they still did even when they already passed. I love them so much. Run free Wanda, Chachi, and Kati."

Helen Simpson shared:

"Beautiful! Absolutely beautiful. My angel was not a cardinal but a white dove. My father passed away in September of 1998. My husband and I rode four-wheelers. We were in the desert riding. He took a ride while I stayed back in our Chevy SUV 4x4. I was sitting on the back tailgate with the front doors open listening to music. I looked up and saw this white dove (there aren't doves in the desert). It flew in one door and out the other. Then it made several circles above me and flew away. When my husband got back, I was balling. I told him the story and I believed it was my dad. Five days later at home, I was on our patio as we lived in the city, there was this big white puffy cloud. I felt a touch on my shoulder but when I turned around, no one was there."

Dawn Allor Godfrey of Michigan shared:

"My beautiful mom passed away suddenly in March 2017, from a stroke which left all of us in a state of sadness. She was a wife, a mom, a grandma, the oldest sister, a loving aunt, and a friend to anyone she met. I loved my mom, but did I really make enough time for her? I lived an hour away and worked part-time. I had the guilt heavy on my heart. How could I ever ask for her forgiveness? I didn't get to say goodbye. This went on inside my heart and it hurt. In March of 2020, I started to have dreams of her. Small snippets, but enough to let me hear her voice or feel like she was with me. It felt good, but it wasn't enough to smooth my heartache. COVID hit me in April 2020 and I was pretty sick. During the middle of the sickness, she came to me when I needed her the most. There she was in my dream as an orb, all willowing, soft, and floating. She took me by my shoulders and held me and didn't let go. All I can say is we melded together where our bodies were as one being. It is so hard to explain the feelings it left. I woke up the next morning and I was on the mend, both physically and

emotionally. My heart was healed. I miss her terribly, and I still pick up the phone to call her, but it doesn't hurt anymore."

Lori Baker (Elle Bee) shared:

"I have been blessed to witness many signs in my life from a higher power, and angels. One of the most mystical and magical experiences came a year before my mother passed away. I was in complete and total awe. After my brother passed away, my mother said I want to move closer to you. She was in assisted living because she needed two people to transport her. She said, 'I am ready to move, but I will miss my ducks, maybe they will come?' I said 'Mom, maybe they will.' She loved feeding the ducks in the courtyard at her assisted living and they loved her back.

The same month I was moving mom, I came home, and a duck made a nest right by our front porch. I couldn't believe it. Cement surrounded this little haven of a shrub and dirt. There she was sitting in her nest. I came in and called mom. I said, 'Mom you will never guess what just happened, a duck came for your arrival.' She was so happy. I named her Greta Gumbo.

Mom got to meet Greta on Memorial Day and it was the last time mom would see her. Greta had her babies and left to take them to water. It was such a magical experience, but it was just the start. My mother passed away a year later. One day I am on the phone talking about Greta and she comes in for a landing in our pool. With her, was her partner, who I named Amazing Larry. They spent most of the summer with us before flying south for the winter.

The next year I was getting food ready for them. It was still very early, almost too early for them to come. My husband says to me, 'So, you think they are coming today?' I said, 'Yes, I felt their presence last night.' He kind of laughed and said, 'ok.' As he grabbed his keys both Greta and Larry came in for a landing. The cover was still on the pool. The look on Jeff's face was priceless. Mine too, I suppose. This was when I truly understood the connections we make with nature and how we are truly one.

For the next few years, I always knew the day they would come. The last one, I said 'Larry will be coming alone' , I knew something happened to my Greta. She passed away and somehow, I knew it. On the day I felt Larry coming, Jeff was on a conference call for work, but he came running upstairs and said, Larry is here.

As life goes, major changes happened and I was called away from that home, but I forever treasure and love my connection with Greta and Amazing Larry. I just know my mom had something to do with this magic."

Chapter 5

"The Healing Journey and Other Musings"

I have always been a seeker in life, I search for the common threads of truth. It is undeniable that we are all connected with each other in an infinite way. Connected to nature, to each other, and to spirit. As my favorite "earth school" teacher Ram Dass once said, "We are all just walking each other home". I will never forget the first time I read it. I had goosebumps and tears welled in my eyes. Our time in this dimension is so limited, but these stories, along with my experiences, have left me with no doubt about our limitless interconnection with our loved ones that have passed on.

When people have sought me out for guidance on grief, I can only say healing is not a linear process. Like life, it has its ups and downs, a three steps forward, two steps backwards dance to it. Surrender to the dance and know the unbearable moments will pass. Be extra kind and patient with yourself and ask those around you for the same. Reach out for support and keep those no longer with you in this dimension alive with memories. Try to leave the bad memories behind knowing everyone was and is doing their best. They are now free and at peace, and they want the same for us. Their love for us now has no condition and it is so freeing that we can return the same to them. Don't beat yourself up with the "I shoulds". "I should have answered the phone that last day", "I should have been a better son, daughter, friend", etc. Expectations leave when we leave the human mind. Isn't that beautiful? Please, my friends, know you were more than enough. All that remains is love.

I am beyond grateful and honored to those of you who shared these amazing stories with me. Together, we can go on a mission to help people heal and connect. For those of you reading this that are grieving, I am truly sorry for your pain. I hope you see your signs soon. They will come. Love truly never dies.

Love, light, and waves of healing –

Lori "Elle Bee" Baker

Made in the USA
Monee, IL
25 July 2022

bb4a2510-5998-46b2-8db5-4c0ef875716dR02